BRASS RUBBING

BRASS RUBBING

Malcolm Norris

PAN BOOKS LONDON AND SYDNEY

First published 1965 by Studio Vista
This edition published 1977 by Pan Books Ltd,
Cavaye Place, London SW10 9PG
© Malcolm Norris 1965
ISBN 0 330 25095 7
Printed in Great Britain by Fletcher & Son Ltd, Norwich

Also available in this series

Crochet   Emily Wildman
Candlemaking   Mary Carey
Jewellery   Thomas Gentille
Pottery   Jolyon Hofsted
Framing   Eamon Toscano
Macramé   Mary Walker Phillips
Rugmaking   Nell Znamierowski
Weaving   Nell Znamierowski
Filography   Douglas K. Dix
Country Crafts   Valerie Janitch
Appliqué   Evangeline Shears & Diantha Fielding
Soft Toys   Mabs Tyler
More Soft Toys   Mabs Tyler
The Art of Dried and Pressed Flowers
    Pamela Westland & Paula Critchley
The Art of Shellcraft   Paula Critchley
Needlework   Winifred Butler
Creative Patchwork   June Field

Contents

Frontispiece Angel bearing a shield, c. 1470.
Flemish work. Nieuportville, Belgium.
Size approx. 30″ x 22″.

PREFACE

A monumental brass is a figure, inscription, shield or other device, engraved in plate brass and laid as a memorial. Such memorials are found throughout central and north western Europe and are a celebrated feature of many English churches. Their origin can be traced to the late twelfth century, a period in which commemoration of the dead by incised stone or sculptured figures became increasingly common.

The craft of bronze and brass casting was highly developed by the twelfth century, and it was not surprising that the metal workers' skill should have been applied to enrich incised stone slabs. Three main factors favoured the development of brasses. Firstly, the metal itself was beautiful in colour, receptive of fine decoration and durable. Secondly, a flat memorial which could be set in the floor created few problems of arrangement or space. Thirdly, a pictorial representation, unlike sculpture, could be varied in size without apparent incongruity. The great historical and artistic value of brasses has arisen from their record of costume, heraldry and social history, as much as from their quality of craftmanship. They are, moreover, the most consistently dated works of art of the Middle Ages. Their value as a source of historical information has been greatly increased by the ease and exact reproduction of their design.

Many books deal with brasses in general or concentrate on the collections in individual counties. This book is a guide to the study of brasses, emphasising the many respects in which the subject remains a challenge. It sets out to reveal brasses as worthy of study in their own right, not merely as an asset to the study of costume and heraldry.

The technique of brass rubbing has been described in detail, as the making of rubbings is usually the accompaniment, and often the starting-point, of a serious interest in brasses. Whatever the collector's motives, the making of good rubbings is important.

An attempt has been made to describe brasses in their European context, and to discard the insular perspective which has prevailed too long. To enthuse over Flemish brasses in England yet ignore those in Belgium is illogical.

This is not intended to be a text book, and its format does not permit the inclusion of long footnotes. Confirmation for the text can be found in the illustrated examples or in the books referred to in the sixth chapter.

1 BRASS RUBBING

The term 'brass rubbing' is applied to a number of processes used to reproduce exactly the engraved design of monumental brasses. The products can be described as monotone rubbings, colour facsimiles and dabbings. The qualities of brasses that facilitate their reproduction are the smoothness of the plate surface and the clear recession of the engraved lines. Rubbing with dark wax on paper laid over the brass causes friction only on the plane surface and consequently reveals the engraved lines as white against a dark background. Certain considerations are relevant to all types of rubbings.

1. *Permission* Brasses are occasionally found in museums and cathedrals, but mostly in parish churches. Wherever they are, it is necessary to obtain permission to make rubbings. In a parish church the priest in charge is responsible and has discretion in granting or witholding permission. The dean controls such matters in a cathedral and the curator in a museum. While difficulty rarely arises, it is both courteous and advisable to request permission in writing. Often church fittings such as carpets have to be disarranged to expose the brasses. In several churches, especially in the vicinity of London and Cambridge, fees are charged, while at other places, Cobham, Kent, and Higham Ferrers, Northants., for example, strict control has been imposed due to the large number of applications. Some brasses are permanently covered with glass, as at Newcastle on Tyne, and others, such as at Dvrham, Gloucestershire, are concealed by the pews. The giving of adequate notice makes a favourable reception probable and prevents a wasted visit.

2. *Accessibility of brasses* Brasses vary in their situation. Many lie in their original positions on the floor (Fig. 1), on the tops of table tombs or vertically at the back of canopied monuments. A considerable number were fixed to the wall during church restoration, and some of these are now at an almost inaccessible height. The important brasses at Warwick and Aldborough, Yorkshire, are only reached with great difficulty. A few brasses are found in unexpected places - at Thaxted, Essex, on the church door (Fig. 2) and at Ringsfield, Suffolk, on an exterior wall. Several English brasses are on slabs in churchyards, while in Nuremberg there are a large number of inscriptions and shields in the old cemeteries.

It is difficult to fix the paper satisfactorily in some of these situations. Floor brasses offer the least problem, as the paper can be held in place by hand or knee without

Fig. 1. A brass in its stone on the floor. Richard Fox, 1439. Arkesden, Essex.

Fig. 2. An inscription, c. 1500, curiously placed on the church door. Thaxted, Essex.

Fig. 3. Brass rubbing at Arkesden. The tension on the paper is under constant hand control.

Fig. 4. A brass on a richly carved table tomb. John Berners and wife, 1523. Finchingfield, Essex.

strain (Fig. 3), or secured with weights or masking tape. Table tomb brasses are similarly convenient, though personal movement is more restricted (Fig. 4). Brasses in a vertical position are more difficult. If the brass is fixed to a soft plaster surface the tape will peel off, marking the plaster, or if it is against a carved and recessed tomb-back there is no suitable surface for fixing the tape (Fig. 5). The help of an assistant is valuable in such cases, and his task will be easier if the paper is rolled at the top on to a stick. It is clear that any shift in the paper will spoil the rubbing.

Most continental brasses are fixed to walls, including the enormous compositions at Schwerin, Germany, Torun, Poland, and the Bruges brasses. The author has found it effective to fix the tape to the top edge of these large rectangular brasses rather than to the walls, as the weight of the paper is too great for the tape to adhere to an irregular surface. No harm is caused by this process and the top edge may be rubbed separately on a small sheet.

3. *Examination and cleaning* All brasses should be care-

Fig. 5. A fine heraldic Tudor brass at the back of a recessed tomb. Sir Robert Clyfford and wife, 1508. Aspenden, Herts.

fully cleaned with a duster and soft brush before rubbing is started. Otherwise grit and dust will distort the result and lead to the tearing of the paper. A final check for dust on brass or slab should be made with the bare hand before laying the paper. Flaws in the surface of the brass should be noted. These consist of protruding rivets, plate joins and the irregularities which are common in sixteenth-century English plate. The brass itself may be set below the level of the slab, or stone decay may have left the brass in relief. None of these features need compromise a rubbing if their presence is realised from the start. Irregular surfaces should be rubbed carefully, raised edges being indicated lightly from the outset, while the overall tension on the paper should be released during the rubbing of recessed detail.

4. *Rubbing methods* The three recommended rubbing processes are different in their nature and result, and require separate treatment.

(a) *Monotone rubbing* Rubbing in monotone, the most commonly used, is the simplest and most effective process. The major national collections of the Society of An-

Fig. 6. Contrast between good and bad rubbings. The rubbing on the right was made in the material recommended. The others were made with cobbler's wax, one carefully and the other carelessly.

tiquaries, London, and the Museum of Archaeology and Ethnology, Cambridge, consist mainly of rubbings of this type.

This process is an old one. The seventeenth-century Dutch artist, H. C. van der Vliet, painted children rubbing incised slabs at Delft. It is possible that in the fifteenth century the engravers used rubbings to produce the remarkable copies described in Chapter 3.

The materials used for the rubbing are black heel-ball and suitable white paper. Heel-ball, a compound of beeswax, tallow and lamp black, is easily obtainable. Unfortunately much is very greasy in texture and marks unevenly (Fig. 6). The best results are obtained by using a special heel-ball, in sticks or cakes, prepared at the request of

13

Fig. 7. The materials used for rubbing.

the Monumental Brass Society and sold exclusively by Phillips and Page Ltd., 50, Kensington Church Street, London. This has a hard and permanent quality. Most of the rubbings illustrated here have been made with it (Fig. 6).

Strong, thin paper of adequate width is necessary. Thick paper decreases the clarity of fine engraving, while narrow strips prove difficult to join exactly. Most paper stretches under the stress of rubbing. The most satisfactory is detail paper, which is obtainable in widths of up to sixty inches and can be bought in shops dealing with architects' and draughtsmen's materials. Good quality lining paper as sold in wallpaper stores is cheaper and perfectly adequate if the brasses are narrow and complicated joins can be avoided.

Many brass rubbers are disappointed by their grey and uneven results. Hard rubbing from the start is necessary to produce an even and black effect, so the collector should be prepared for strenuous exercise. A dull point should be kept on the wax. Most controlled pressure can be obtained if the shoulders are kept above and over the working wrist, and if the body position is changed to facilitate the rubbing of a particular portion. It is not essential to rub in one direction only. It is important to rub systematically, as subsequent work on half-finished sections may reveal distortions caused by paper expansion. A cake of heel-ball which can be manipulated with both hands is often more effective for large expanses than a small stick.

There are circumstances where it is advisable to rub the whole stone slab, and some collectors do this as a matter

of course. The stone indents from which brasses have been lost are important to the composition. A blunt stick of heel-ball is best for this work, and a circular rubbing action is effective. Moderate pressure only should be used.

A final polish should be given with a duster before the paper is removed.

(b) *Colour facsimiles*   If a rubbing is required solely for decoration, a colour facsimile may be made to display the pleasing colour relationship of the brass to its slab. The process has the merit of defining the engraved lines as black, which is true to the original design.

A special 'metallic' rubber was invented in the nineteenth century for use with dark grey paper. The rubbings made with this were dramatic but lacked precision. A similar but more accurate effect may be achieved by using a brown or yellow heel-ball. The rubbing is made in the manner already described, but after completion the paper is wiped with waterproof black ink. The ink will stain only the lines, being resisted by the waxy surface of the heel-ball. The rubbing is then cut out and mounted on grey paper, and any heraldic features painted with tempera. The detail in colour facsimiles is rarely as sharp as in monotone rubbings. The process is therefore only recommended for its decorative quality (Fig. 9).

An alternative but more laborious process is to remove the wax. This may be done if a poor quality heel-ball is used. The rubbing should be made initially with a coloured heel-ball, the lines being darkened with black ink which is allowed to dry. Subsequently the rubbing is wiped with a paraffin-soaked rag which effectively disintegrates the surface of the heel-ball. Colour may then be applied according to taste. The darkening of the lines with accuracy requires both care and skill.

(c) *Dabbing*   A dabbing is made with a pad and graphite. The pad is formed of a piece of chamois leather wrapped round cotton-wool. Powdered graphite is mixed with linseed oil into a paste on a small board. After the pad has been dipped into the paste, and surplus paste has been wiped off, it is applied with moderate pressure to the surface of the paper. Very little friction is caused and so it is possible to use very thin paper, such as tissue paper.

The contrast between white and black in a dabbing is not great, but the fineness of the paper secures the impression of all recessions (Fig. 8). The process is accordingly suitable for copying brasses with intricate or shallow engraving. It has also proved effective for use on indents, where the stone surface may be too uneven for a monotone rubbing. Dabbing of a slab or indent can be combined effectively with monotone rubbing of the brass inlays.

(d) *Other rubbing methods*   Other ways of making rubbings have been tried but they have proved less satisfactory than those described. The most interesting is the technique of the eighteenth-century antiquaries, Craven Ord and Sir John Cullum, who made a large collection including the only record of many brasses since lost. Their facsimiles were produced by pressing wet paper on to the surface of the brass after the lines had been flooded with printers' ink. They are still remarkably clear, although the design is shown in reverse. The collection is now in the British Museum. Permission for such a process would hardly be granted in the twentieth century!

5. *Rubbings made for public record*

Certain standards have been set for rubbings preserved in public collections, and these should be adhered to if a collection is made for historical record. A rubbing should record the exact relationship of all parts of the brass and the indents of missing portions. Rivet holes should be marked in indents where possible. The rubbing should be of the best quality and should not be remounted. The date on which the rubbing was made, the place, the position in the church and particulars of the persons represented should be recorded on the paper. All these details may prove of importance in the course of later research. Any tears arising should be repaired with paper and paste and not with plastic tape, which may in time stain the paper.

6. *Retouching*

The use of waterproof black ink for retouching can be recommended if the rubbing is to be used for reproduction or decoration. The ink should be applied to even or intensify a good rubbing, or to eliminate marks that have arisen accidentally through fragments of dirt. Extensive retouching of a poor rubbing is most unsatisfactory, as errors are invariably made. If remounting is required, linen is a good backing for large rubbings and cardboard for small ones.

7. *Arrangement of a collection*

Most collections are arranged in alphabetical order, according to church and county. This method is suitable for quick reference and new items can be added easily. Arrangement according to type or period is more complicated, but it is better for study purposes especially if comparing costumes. The most valuable arrangement for

Fig. 9. A colour facsimile of Sir John d Wautone and wife, 1347. Wimbish, Essex Length of male effigy 19½".

original research is to attempt groupings by engraving styles. This presupposes a large collection and good knowledge of the subject by the collector. The groupings may lack certainty, but they will open excellent prospects for the kind of investigation which is described in Chapter 3.

8. *Storage of a collection*

A large collection of rubbings presents a considerable problem of storage. Provided the rubbings are not required for exhibition, the best solution is to store them in folders. Strong folders can be made of thick cardboard or hardboard, with sides of canvas or linen. The rubbings can be folded to size and protected completely. This arrangement is ideal for small examples.

The folding of rubbings is unsatisfactory if they are to be used for exhibition. Multiple creases spoil the overall effect. A good alternative is to roll the rubbings within cardboard tubes. Ideal tubes for the purpose are used for the package of plastic material and linoleum, and these can be obtained in bulk from furnishing stores. Phillips and Page Limited arrange the retail sale of such tubes. These, with the contents clearly marked on the outside, can be easily stacked.

9. *The photographing of rubbings*

Many collectors find a selection of photographs of rubbings very valuable for reference. They save much wear and tear on the original rubbings. These, however, are not easy objects to photograph. Apart from problems of size, there is usually much subtle variation in the blackness of a rubbing, and reflected light from the waxy surface can prove extremely troublesome. The best results for the amateur can be obtained by taking photographs out of doors on a dull day, the rubbings being mounted on a fence or wall. Strong direct light is to be avoided.

Professional skill is required if the photographs are to be used for publication. Printing techniques decide the final result almost as much as the quality of the negative.

It is necessary to conclude with a point previously made — that brass rubbing is not a public right. The discretion of the incumbent must be respected, and the property of the church must be equally respected. Far too often irresponsible people have caused offence by misusing church equipment and ignoring the vicar's authority. Such actions compromise the position of the serious student. It is the author's conviction that an informed public interest in brasses can be a valuable influence for the better care and preservation of brasses. This interest must be tempered with care and respect.

2 THE COMMEMORATED

No aspect of monumental brasses has attracted such interest as the persons represented. From the figures of the commemorated has been drawn the record of costume, armour and custom, for which brasses are famous. Brasses have little value as personal portraits. The engravers represented types, not individuals, and the features of one brass will usually be found repeated on many others. Portrait brasses are found after the mid-sixteenth century, but even then they are in the minority. The series of plates to the Ducal House of Saxony at Freiberg, Germany, are based on actual likenesses. Nicholas and Dorothie Wadham (1618) at Ilminster, Somerset (Fig. 31) and Samuel Harsnett (1631) at Chigwell, Essex, are undoubtedly attempts at portraiture. Age or personal characteristics were often indicated by features which contrasted with the current convention, such as the long beard of Sir William Tendring (1408) at Stoke by Nayland, Suffolk, or the streaming hair of Joan Kniveton (c.1485) at Mugginton, Derbyshire.

Occasionally an individual is identified by some article or situation. William Palmer 'with ye stylt' (1520) at Ingoldmells, Lincs., is shown with his crutch beside him (Fig. 10). The brass of Sir William Molineux (c.1570) at Sefton, Lancs., includes the banners this knight captured at Floddon Field. More curiously, John Selwyn (1587) at Walton-on-Thames, Surrey, is engraved riding a stag, a feat of agility he performed in the presence of Queen Elizabeth I. Robert Wyvil, Bishop of Salisbury (1375) at Salisbury, is represented praying within the castle of Sherborne, which he recovered for the church (Fig. 11). The Chase of Bere which he also recovered is indicated by warrens and rabbits, while the bishop's champion is shown standing at the castle gate with a rectangular shield and war hammer.

The value of brasses as a record of human affairs lies mainly in the strata of society represented. All classes of society from royalty to modest traders used brasses for their memorials. A summary of the main classes represented and their distinctive dress is valuable both for its own interest and as a guide to the dating of brasses. What follows, however, is no more than a brief introduction to a fascinating study.

1. *Royalty*

There are three existing brasses to royalty. By far the finest is the Flemish brass to King Eric Menved of Denmark (died 1319) and his Queen Ingeborg at Ringstead,

Fig. 10. William Palmer 'with ye stylt' 1520. Ingoldmells, Lincs. Length of effigy 20".

Fig. 11. Robert Wyvil, Bishop of Salisbury, in the castle of Sherborne, 1375. Salisbury Cathedral, Wilts. Total length 90″. Illustration from Waller.

Fig. 12. King Eric Menved and queen, 1319. Ringstead, Denmark. Length 114″. Flemish work. Illustration from Creeny.

Denmark (Fig. 12). The king and queen are both shown crowned. Both hold sceptres and the king in addition holds a sword over the right shoulder. The remarkable feature of King Eric's dress is a long, sleeveless tunic embroidered with the hearts and crowned lions of the Danish arms. Queen Ingeborg wears a close fitting under dress, the kirtle, over which is a looser garment, the cote-hardie, and a mantle. A curious English example to Ethelred, King of the West Saxons (died 871, but engraved c. 1440), is a small half-figure. The king wears a crown and holds a sceptre (Fig. 75). His dress is a

Fig. 13. Duke Premizlaus of Steinau, c. 1300. Lubiaz Poland. Length 100″.

Fig. 14. Sir John D'Abernon, 1277. Stoke D'Abernon, Surrey. Length 78″.

close-sleeved undergarment, a plain mantle and a cape of ermine. Queen Agnes of Sweden (1432) at Gadebusch, Germany, is a large but poorly engraved figure, showing the queen in a loose robe with baggy sleeves and a veil covering her head. Several fine brasses to French royalty have been recorded in drawings. The finest, from St Denis, was to Marguerite of Provence, wife of St Louis (died 1285). Her dress was similar to that of Queen Inge-borg (Fig. 12).

2. *Military figures*

It was customary to represent lords and knights as arm-ed, and accordingly military figures cover a large sect-ion of society, ranging from dukes of Saxony to small English landowners and squires. The record of armour so preserved is particularly valuable for the period 1270 to 1450, as little actual armour has survived from these years. Changes in style are clearly defined, and greatly facilitate the dating of figures.

The years 1270 to 1310 marked the close of the age of mail. Armour was constructed of interlinked riveted iron rings. These are represented on brasses by careful-ly defined links or bands of semi-circular crescents. The mail armour consisted of a long shirt or hawberk, a hood or coif, and stockings. The sleeves of the hawberk ex-tended into mittens. A linen surcoat was worn over the armour. A long cross-hilt sword hung at the waist on a loose belt. Additional protection was provided by a great helm which completely covered the head and a shield. Single spiked spurs were generally used.

This equipment is well represented by the few but choice brasses of the period. Three Polish examples at Lubiaz show the mail without reinforcement, but reveal the gambeson, the padded garment worn beneath to prevent chafing. One of these, Duke Premizlaus of Steinau, has his coif thrown back, revealing his ducal coronet (Fig. 13). The English examples (Figs. 14, 15, 16, 17) at Stoke d'Abernon, Surrey (died 1277), Trumpington, Cambs. (1289), Acton, Suffolk (1302) and Chartham, Kent (d. 1306), are exceptionally well executed, while two half-effigies (c.1300) at Buslingthorpe and Croft, Lincs. (Fig. 99), are interesting. The complete figures show an additional defence – poleyns, knee defences of decorated leather. Sir Robert de Septvans at Chartham is shown bareheaded, his mittens hanging loose and his surcoat embroidered with winnowing fans. The lance is held by the Stoke d'Abernon and Lubiaz (Duke Boleslaus) knights. Appropriate arms are emblazoned on the shields. Herald-ic shoulder wings or 'ailettes' are shown on some of the

Fig. 16. Sir Robert de Bures, 1302. ·Acton, Suffolk. Length 79½″.

Fig. 17. Sir Robert de Septvans, d. 1306. Chartham, Kent. Length 76″.

Fig. 18. Sir John (?) de Northwood, c. 1330. Minster, Isle of Sheppey, Kent. Legs restored c. 1500. Length 71″. Possibly French work. Rubbing by H. F. Owen Evans.

Fig. 19. William Wenemaer. 1325. Museum de Bijloke, Ghent, Belgium. Length 81″. Flemish work.

Fig. 20. Sir John de Cobham, c. 1365.
Canopy omitted. Cobham, Kent. Length of
figure 60″

Fig. 21. Sir Nicholas Hawberk, 1407. Cobham, Kent.
Total length 91″.

2. Helmet of Sir John Mauleverere, Allerton Mauleverer, Yorks. Detail.

figures. Their representation illustrates the limitations of the engravers, as manuscripts show these wings to have been attached to the side of the shoulder, and visible from the side and not the front. The Great Helm is shown behind the head of Sir Roger de Trumpington. Sir Richard de Buslingthorpe wears mittens constructed of scales.

The period 1310 to 1350 marked a transition from mail to plate armour, and brasses show a variety of ingenious and ornamental defences. At Pebmarsh, Essex (1323), and Gorleston, Suffolk (c.1320), appear iron shin defences, 'greaves', and arm defences, 'vambraces and rerebraces'. Sir John de Creke (1325) at Westley Waterless, Cambs. (Fig. 86), shows an early pointed helmet, the bascinet, with its pendant mail neck defence, the aventail. His shortened surcoat reveals the mail shirt and gambeson beneath. His spurs are of rowel or wheel form. Similar figures at Stoke d'Abernon (1327) and Minster in Sheppey, Kent (c.1330), (Fig. 18), show minor differences. William Wenemaer at the Museum de Bijloke, Ghent, Belgium, is a fine Flemish example, showing chains securing both sword and dagger (Fig. 19). The period closes with the remarkable brass of Sir Hugh Hastings (1347) at Elsing, Norfolk, who lies surrounded with armed 'weepers' (Fig. 107). Among many interesting details shown are the iron gorget defence for the neck,

3. Battle scene from brass of St Henry of Finland, c. 1430. Nausis, Finland. Detail. Flemish work. Illustration from mental Brass Society portfolio.

Fig. 24. Sir John Harsick and wife, 1384.
Southacre, Norfolk. Length of the knight
61″.

Fig. 25. Thomas de Cruwe and wife, 1411.
Wixford, Warwick. Total length 108″.

the visors of the helmets, the studded brigandine defence
for the thighs and the broad-brimmed 'war hat' of Alme-
ric Lord St Amand among the weepers. Two smaller
examples in Essex, at Wimbish and Bowers Gifford, illustrate variations on this armour, the latter holding a
gorgeous shield emblazoned with fleur de lys.

During the period 1350 to 1410 armour achieved a more
uniform design, the most consistent features being the
tight-fitting jupon, the successor of the surcoat, the bascinet and aventail, complete plate defences for arms,
legs and feet, and an elaborate belt, the baldrick, supporting the sword and dagger. Examples are numerous.
Sir John de Cobham at Cobham is typical of c. 1365, with
heavy gauntlets and studded thighs (Fig. 20). Sir Nicholas Hawberk (1407) at the same church shows the

Fig.26. Sallet helmet of John Teringham, 1484. Tyringham, Bucks. Detail.

Fig. 27. Sir Kuno von Liebensteyn, 1391. Nowemiasto, Poland. Length 98″. Made at the Marienburg, Poland.

smoother lines armour had developed by the end of the century (Fig. 21). Some unusually interesting features depicted are the highly decorative leg armour of Thomas Cheyne (1368) and the fish scale foot armour or sabbatons of William Cheyne (1375), both at Drayton Beauchamp, Bucks.; the pointed visor of John Mauleverere (1400) at Allerton Mauleverer, Yorks. (Fig. 22) and the superb baldrick of John de St Quintin at Brandsburton, Yorks. A dramatic pitched battle of the close of this period is shown on two side panels of the brass to St Henry of Finland (c. 1430) at Nausis, Finland. Axes, glaives, cross bows, spears and a cannon are among the weapons of the contestants (Fig. 23). Continental figures usually show weapons chained to the breastplate, or brigandine, beneath the jupon.

Many jupons are embroidered with heraldic devices. Fine English examples are at Fletching, Sussex (1380), Aldborough, Yorks . (1360), Southacre, Norfolk (1384) (Fig. 24), Letheringham (1389) and Playford, Suffolk (1400). The most elaborate is that of Thomas de Beauchamp, Earl of Warwick (1406) at St Mary's, Warwick, on which the charges are delicately stippled. A unique example is the brass of Kuno von Liebensteyn (1391) at Nowemiasto, Poland, who is armed as a knight of the Teutonic crusader order (Fig. 27). The cross is emblazoned on his jupon, mantle and great rectangular shield or pavise.

From 1410 to 1490 all-plate armour was developed in a variety of beautiful and effective styles. A good transitional example is that of William Willoughby D'Eresby (1410) at Spilsby, Lincs. (Fig. 89), showing the plate gorget covering the aventail and the fauld or skirt of plate protecting the pelvis. The jewelled orle round the helmet is a rare feature. Thomas de Cruwe (1411), Wixford, Warwick., wears complete plate armour in a fashion which remained stable till 1430 (Fig. 25). The rounded bascinet, gorget, palettes at the armpits, sword and gauntlets are all typical. Equally fine examples are at Felbrigg, Norfolk (1416), and Trotton, Sussex (1419). A mace hangs at the hip of Nicholas Maudyt (1420) at Wandsworth, Surrey.

A change of style about 1440 reflects the influence of Milanese armourers. Heavy pauldrons were added to protect the shoulders, the armour of the left elbow was reinforced (Fig. 1), and small thigh guards or tassets were attached to the fauld. Richard Dixton (1438) at Cirencester, Glos., is a clear example of these changes. Another variation of the armour, in which the fauld is long and the arm defences kept symmetrical, is shown in a group of brasses of which Hugh Halsham (1441) at West Grinstead, Sussex, is typical.

From 1460 to 1485 the gothic style of armour, associated with the superb armours of the Colmans of Augsburg, is generally depicted. The line of the armour was forged to form a series of pointed ridges. The breastplate was reinforced and a distinctive visored helmet, the sallet, was worn in conjunction with a beaver to protect the chin and throat. This style is well illustrated, the best example being at Tong, Salop. (1467) (Fig. 28). The sallet is clearly shown without the beaver at Tyringham, Bucks (1484) (Fig. 26), and with the beaver at Stokesby, Norfolk (1488). The sword is usually placed across the front of the body.

Fig. 28. Sir William Vernon and wife, 1467. Tong, Salop. Total length 76″. Illustration from Waller.

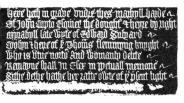

g. 29. Edward Sulyard and wife, c. 1495.
igh Laver, Essex. Total length 39″.

Heraldic tabards became a common feature during this period. The tabard was a loose garment with wide sleeves emblazoned with heraldic arms, and was the successor of the earlier heraldic surcoats and jupons. Henry Grene of Drayton (1467) at Lowick, Northants., is an attractive example (Fig. 109).

During a short period of transition from 1485 to 1495 the pointed forms of the gothic style became rounded and less graceful, and from 1495 to 1550 armour is shown in a variety of clumsy fashions. The sabbatons are rounded and broad, the pauldrons are large with high hautepieces to protect the neck, and the thighs are protected by a mail skirt and long tassets. A lance rest is often riveted to the breastplate (Fig. 29). Helmets are rarely shown worn, though tilting helms with crest and manteling are used as cushions for the head. John Borrell (1531) at Broxbourne, Herts., is an exception, wearing a close helmet with visor raised. A general deterioration of workmanship added to the ugliness of the representation, and much of the armour is inaccurately rendered. English examples of the period are very numerous, those at Hunstanton, Norfolk (1506), Wivenhoe, Essex (1507), Hillingdon, Middx. (1509), and Middle Claydon, Bucks. (1542), being the best. Continental examples are superior. Albert, Duke of Saxony (1500) at Meissen, Germany, wearing a sallet and holding a banner, is particularly good. Jehan de Likerke (1518) at Bruges Cathedral and Louis Cortewille (1504) at the Victoria and Albert Museum, London, are Flemish brasses showing the armour in accurate detail. The most surprising example is that of Nicholas Tomiczki (1524) at Tomice, Poland. He is shown standing in a ridged and slashed parade suit with the banner he carried as ensign of Poznan (Fig. 74). Tabards are commonly shown up to 1550. Sir Ralph Verney (1547) at Aldbury, Herts., is a good illustration (Fig. 30).

Armour became of less practical importance during the latter half of the sixteenth century, but was usually represented for show. The breastplate was of peascod form, the tassets were long and laminated, and the pauldrons were broad and humped. The two finest English examples are at St Decumans (1596) and Ilminster (1618) (Fig. 31), both in Somerset. Continental armours are shown in more decorative forms, the armour of the Freiberg dukes being profusely etched. The earliest, Duke Henry the Pious (1541), is armed in the style of a mercenary with a deep mail hood – the 'Bishop's Mantle' – and two-handed sword.

During the first half of the seventeenth century part-armour was widely used. Sir Edward Filmer (1629) at East Sutton, Kent, wears a breastplate, gorget, arm defences and rectangular tassets, while his legs are protected by high boots. Ralph Assheton (1650) at Middleton, Lancs., is similarly armed (Fig. 32). As late as c.1630 Richard Barttelot of Stopham, Sussex, is shown in complete plate (Fig. 34). Nevertheless by 1640 suits of armour had entirely lost their functional value. The power of the musket and the need for speed on the battlefield rendered armour obsolete. The record of military brasses may be aptly concluded with the kneeling figure of Alfred Brockman at Cheriton, Kent, in the khaki battledress of the First World War.

Some military figures wear badges or collars or carry emblems of office which add greatly to their interest. The two most important decorations are the collar and pendant of the Order of the Golden Fleece and the inscribed garter of the Most Noble Order of the Garter. The former was established by Philip the Good, Duke of Burgundy, at Bruges in 1430. The collar with its pendant replica of the fleece is well illustrated on the brass of Philip's wife, Isabella (c.1450), now at the Archaeological Museum, Basel, Switzerland. The Order of the Garter was founded by Edward III in 1349 and six brasses to knights of this order exist. The most elaborate is that of Sir Thomas Bullen (1538) at Hever, Kent, who wears the full insignia of the Order, including the mantle with badge and collar of garters (Fig. 33). The garter itself is shown below the left knee of the knights. Among other decorations the blue collar bearing the repeated letter S, awarded by the House of Lancaster, is commonly found on English brasses of knights and ladies from 1400 to 1460 and again in the early sixteenth century (Fig. 41). The red Yorkist collar of suns and roses created by Edward IV occurs on brasses from 1465 to 1490. The crown badge of a Yeoman of the Crown is engraved on the left shoulder of a figure (c.1480) in the possession of the Society of Antiquaries, London. Thomas, Lord Berkeley (1392), at Wotton-under-Edge, Glos., wears a family collar of mermaids. Sir Symon Felbrygge K.G., banner bearer to Richard II, is represented with the royal banner at Felbrigg, Norfolk. John Borrell, Sergeant at Arms to Henry VIII, at Broxbourne, Herts., holds a ceremonial mace.

Fig. 30. Sir Ralph Verney and wife, 15.. Aldbury., Herts. Total length 85".

3. *Civilian brasses*

The majority of English brasses depict persons in civilian dress. A great proportion of these represent undistinguished people, and the brasses themselves are often

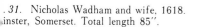

31. Nicholas Wadham and wife, 1618.
Ilminster, Somerset. Total length 85".

small and lack detail. Nevertheless the memorials of the great merchants, especially the English wool traders, are among the finest in existence. Continental examples are few in number and this summary is principally based on English evidence.

Male civil costume from 1300 to 1410 is shown as consisting of a sleeved tunic, a chaperon covering the shoulders, hose and pointed shoes. John Pecok at St Michael's, St Alban's, is a simple example which probably dates from c. 1340 (Fig. 35). In some cases, such as Robert Braunche (1364) at King's Lynn, Norfolk, long pendants hang from the sleeves and the tight sleeves of an undergarment can be seen. Occasionally the tunic is buttoned, as on Robert de Paris (1408) at Hildersham, Cambs. (Fig. 116). A farmer (c.1370) at Shottesbrooke, Berks., illustrates another variant in which the tunic is belted and a mantle buttoned on the right shoulder is worn. A short sword or basilard often hangs from the belt.

Until 1350 women are generally represented in simple dress. Lady Joan de Cobham (c.1320) at Cobham, wears a kirtle with buttoned sleeves under the cote hardie (Fig. 108). A kerchief or veil covers her head, and a wimple covers her chin and throat. The cote hardie of Margarete de Camoys at Trotton, Sussex (c.1310), is decorated with shields (Fig. 36). Alyne de Creke (1325) at Westley Waterless, Cambs., wears a mantle. Flemish and German brasses follow the same pattern, though the kirtle on several Flemish examples, Margaret de Walsokne (1349) at King's Lynn being one, is very richly embroidered. The dress of Elizabeth (?) de Northwood (c.1335) at Minster in Sheppey, Kent, is most peculiar, displaying a voluminous gorget. An interesting change of fashion after 1350 was to the sideless cote hardie as worn by Elizabeth, Countess of Athol (1375), at Ashford, Kent. Many women wore cote hardies with long pendants similar to those of the men (Fig. 117). Heraldic embroidery on the cote hardie is well illustrated at Southacre, Norfolk (1384), and Bray, Berks (1378) (Fig. 117). The headdress of this period is varied. The veiled headdress consisted of two kerchiefs, one binding the forehead and the other falling over the head to the shoulders. Another form consisted of a series of close caps or cauls enclosing the hair, which is represented on brasses either as a nebulé or zig-zag pattern (Fig. 37). The reticulated headdress, binding the hair in jewelled network, is illustrated at Spilsby, Lincs. (1391), while yet another arrangement showing the hair plaited at the sides and bound occurs at Southacre (1384).

The costume of widows, which remained unchanged until the sixteenth century, consisted of the kirtle, cote hardie and mantle, and the veiled headdress with a wimple and plaited gorget or barbe. A fine representation is on the figure of Eleanor de Bohun (1399), Duchess of Gloucester, at Westminster Abbey (Fig. 38).

English fashions changed at the turn of the fifteenth century. The male tunic was now worn long and loose with a high buttoned collar, and its sleeves became baggy while remaining tight at the wrists. John Urban (1420) at Southfleet, Kent, is a good example. Occasionally the sleeves took an extravagant form, imitating those of the clerical surplice. The mantle and baselard are less frequently shown. After 1420 a fur lining is often represented at the cuffs and hem of the tunic, and laced ankle boots cover the feet. More exotic costumes with decorated sleeves and elongated shoes are recorded on a group of German brasses at Nordhausen.

Female dress followed the pattern of the male, with similar baggy or surplice-like sleeves. The buttoned collar as worn by Marion Grevel (1401) at Chipping Camden, Glos., (Fig. 39), was replaced by a deep-falling collar, well illustrated by Joan Peryent (1415) at Digswell, Herts. (Fig. 41). The sideless cote hardie remained fashionable until 1420, and between 1420 and 1450 the combination of gown and mantle is often shown on brasses. Margaret Cheyne (1419) at Hever, Kent, is a graceful example of the latter style. The greatest changes in female dress were in the headdress. From 1400 to 1420 the hair was usually gathered into nets on either side of the face and over the forehead. A veil fixed over the top, hung down behind. This arrangement is known as the crespine headdress and is finely illustrated by Julian Cruwe (1411) at Wixford (Fig. 25). A change in fashion about 1420 favoured the moulding of the netted hair into great horns over which the veil was hung. Amice Cottusmore (1439) at Brightwell Baldwin, Oxon., is typical of this creation, which is appropriately called the horned headdress (Fig. 51). Various forms of the veil headdress remained in use. Individual extravagances are represented. Joan Peryent at Digswell has her hair arranged in a great triangle above the head (Fig. 41).

Heraldic devices are shown embroidered on both kirtle and mantle, but examples are few before 1470. Elizabeth Fynderne (1444) at Childrey, Berks., is the most decorative.

The costume of the period 1460 to 1490 as shown on brasses is distinctive. The man's tunic is worn to ankle

Fig. 32. Ralph Assheton, 1650. Middle Lancs. Length 18". Wife and family omit

. 33. Sir Thomas Bullen, Knight of the
~~ter~~, 1538. Hever, Kent. Length 60″. In-
~~~~ption omitted.

length and better described as a gown. Its sleeves are
full but not baggy, and a low stiff collar covers the
throat. A belt from which hang a rosary and bag is usually worn. By 1485 shoes have rounded in the toe. John
Lambard (1487), Alderman of London, at Hinxworth,
Herts., is an excellent example of this costume, and
wears a fur lined mantle in addition (Fig. 42). An interesting feature is a cap or hood which is occasionally
shown on the shoulder. This is most clearly shown on
Thomas Kyllegrew (1485) at St Gluvias, Cornwall.
Women are usually shown wearing a fur lined gown over
the kirtle. This gown is cut low at the neck and has tight
fitting sleeves with large cuffs reaching the knuckles.
The horns of the headdress almost meet, giving the arrangement the aspect of a mitre. The headdress peculiar to
the period is the 'butterfly', in which the hair is brushed
back into nets and the veil is extended on wire wings. Its
form is clearly shown as the ladies' heads are often represented in profile. The mitre form of the horns is well
illustrated by Catherine Arderne (1467) at Latton (Harlow), Essex, and the butterfly headdress by Margaret
Bernard (1484), wife of Thomas Peyton, at Isleham,
Cambs. (Fig. 43). The latter is a gorgeous figure, her
gown being completely embroidered and her hair net
inscribed 'Ihu mercy lady help'. Unusual forms of
headdress are the decorated cauls and coronet worn by
Joyce, Lady Tiptoft (c.1470) at Enfield, Middx., and the
spotted horse-shoe shaped bourrelet veil worn by Jane
Keriell (d. 1455) at Ash next Sandwich, Kent.

Heraldically decorated kirtles and mantles became
more common. Both are worn by two ladies (c.1480) at
Long Melford, Suffolk.

Some particularly fine costume is illustrated by Ger-
man and Flemish brasses of this period. John Lünerborch (1474) at St Catherine, Lübeck, wears an exceeding-
ly elaborate fur gown, bag and dagger (Fig. 110). The
Dukes of Saxony, Frederic (1464) and Ernst (d.1486), at
Meissen, wear ermine tippets and tall caps of office. The
maiden Catherine d'Aut (1460) at St Jacques, Bruges, is
a most delicate figure with streaming hair and jewelled
coronet (Fig. 44).

After a brief period of transition, around 1490 new
fashions are depicted. The men wear a fur lined gown
clearly open down the front, with baggy sleeves and
wide collar and cuffs (Fig. 46). The gown is belted at
the waist.

The women's gown is similar to that of the preceeding
period, but square cut at the neck. A long ornamental

SVB HOC IN DÑO REQESCIT MARMOR RICVS BARTTELOT AR, HERES & NEPOS GVLIELMI BARTI
TELOT AR, EX FILIO SVO VNICO ROBTO & MARIA CONIVGE EI (FILIA NATV MAXIMA IOHIS APSLEY
DE THAKEHAM AR.)Q RICVS E MARIA î VXOR (FILIA NATV MIA RICÎ COVERT DE SLAVGHAM AR
4OR FILIOS, & VÑA FILIA, SCLT GVALTERV, EDRV, GVLIELMV, IOHEM, & ANNA & EX ALA
TERA CONIVGE ROESIA (FILIA RICÎ HATTON DE THAMISDITTON IN COM SVRREY
AR) 2OS FILIOS & TOTIDEM FILIAS, VIZ. RICV, ROBTV, MARIA & FRANCISCA, SVSCE
PIT & EX HAC VITA 6TO DIE IVNII AÑ: ÆTAT SVÆ 50 ANNO, DÑI 1614, VER
HVIO ECCLIÆ DE STOPHAM IN COM SVSSEX PATRONVS MIGRAVIT.

Fig. 34. Richard Barttelot and wives, c. 1630.
Stopham, Sussex. Total length 70″.

Fig. 35. John Pekok and wife, c. 13-
Michael's, St Albans, Herts.
Length of figures 35″.

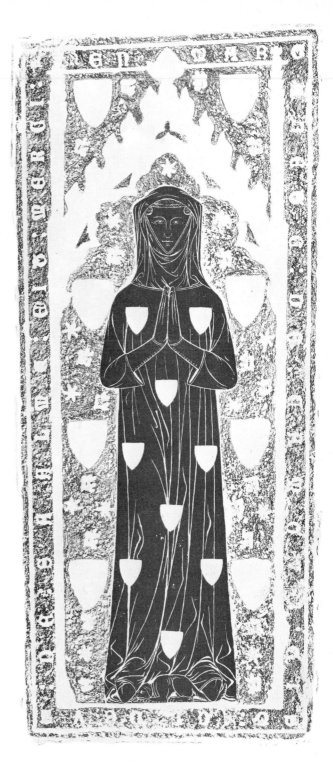

Fig. 36. Margarete de Camoys, c. 1310. Trotton, Sussex. Length 84″. Rubbing by R. Greenwood.

girdle is generally worn, often with a clasp of three roses. The fashionable headdress is distinctive, consisting of a cap and veil with a broad decorative band or frontlet falling from the top on to the shoulders. This is known as the pedimental or kennel headdress. Examples of this dress are very numerous. Continental examples, in particular those at Bruges, differ in the extreme looseness of the sleeves and the use of a veil headdress. The dress of Ellyn, wife of Andrew Evyngar (1535), at All Hallows, Barkyng, London, is an example of Flemish origin.

Minor changes of fashion are represented between 1525 and 1550. The men's gown alters in form. Instead of passing the arms through the length of the sleeve, slits are made at elbow level through which the arms are passed. The remainder of the sleeve is left as a decoration or false sleeve. The gown is often shown open, revealing the doublet and hose beneath. Shoes are often represented as flat in the toe. Henry Hatche (1533) at Faversham, Kent, is typical, and Thomas Pownder (1525) at the Museum, Ipswich, is an excellent Flemish example (Fig. 45).

The women's gown was also changed, and the sleeves are shown full and short, revealing the finely decorated and slashed sleeves of the under garment. The partlet, a linen garment of pleated material, is visible at the neck, and the frontlet of the headdress is doubled back. A long rosary usually takes the place of the girdle. A celebrated example of this costume is Elizabeth Perepoynt (1543) at West Malling, Kent, though most of the features are equally well shown on the brass of Anne Danvers (1539) at Dauntsey, Wilts. (Fig. 47). There are many variants to the costume during these last two periods. A flat cap is worn by women on brasses near Cambridge and Bedford, and a sash takes the place of the girdle. East Anglian brasses often show the women's gowns caught up in front or behind, and a pomander or bag hangs from the girdle.

Heraldic mantles are represented until 1560, Elizabeth Verney (1547) at Aldbury, Herts. (Fig. 30), being a good late instance. Elizabeth Gorynge (1558) at Burton, Sussex, is a curious case, as she is shown in a tabard and not a mantle.

Male fashions from 1550 to 1610 were based on the gown with false sleeves and the doublet and hose. Ralph Hawtrey (1574) at Ruislip, Middx., showing the striped sleeves and doublet, is typical (Fig. 48). Small ruffs are shown at the neck and wrists. Padded breeches − trunk hose − were worn, and hose for the legs.

Fig. 37. Nebulé headdress of Elizab Countess of Athol, 1375. Ashford, K Detail.

Fig. 38. Eleanor de Bohun, 1399. Westminster Abbey. Length 102".

Fig. 39. William Grevel and wife, 1401. Chipping Campden, Glos. Total length 108".

Winifred Hawtrey illustrates the main features of female dress. Her gown is short sleeved and open from the waist, revealing the under sleeves and skirt of the undergown or petticoat respectively. This skirt is often shown elaborately embroidered. Small ruffs are worn at the neck and wrists. The form of her headdress, known ·as the French hood, consists of a wired cap, slightly depressed over the brow, and a veil. A particularly fine example of this style is an unknown lady (c.1580) at Staplehurst, Kent. Brasses to women at the close of the sixteenth century often show stiff outstanding ruffs, tall hats and the skirt extended by the farthingale, the forerunner of the crinoline. The farthingale is superbly illustrated by Duchess Sybella Elizabeth (1606) at Freiberg (Fig. 49).

Fig. 40. Early horned headdress of Elizabeth, Lady Camoys, 1419. Trotton, Sussex. Detail.

Fig. 42. John Lambard and wife, Hinxworth, Herts. Length of male 45″.

Fig. 41. Unusual headdress of Joan Peryent, 1415. Digswell, Herts. Detail.

43. Margaret Peyton, 1484. Isleham, bs. Length 28". Detail from brass of nas Peyton and wives.

The replacement of ruffs by falling collars, often decorated with lace, is a feature of dress after 1610. Men's cloaks are generally shown shorter in length, and rapiers are often worn. Women are usually shown in gowns with puffed sleeves, often decorated with ribbons. Their shoes are high-heeled, in contrast to late sixteenth-century fashion. The wives of Richard Barttelot at Stopham, Sussex, and the daughters of Sir Edward Filmer (1629) at East Sutton, Kent, are illustrations (Fig. 50). Brasses engraved after 1650 are of little value to the student of costume. The debased figures of Benjamin and Philadelphia Greenwood at St Mary Cray, Kent, indicate the costume of the eighteenth century.

In addition to being a guide to costume, civilian brasses give a good indication of men's hair styles, as hats are rarely worn. Brasses from 1300 to 1360 show the hair worn long, and beards and moustaches are common. The beards are sometimes double-pointed. From 1370 to 1410 the hair is generally shown cut short on the head. From 1410 to 1475 the great majority of figures are clean shaven with their hair cut short and rolled. From 1475 to 1550 the hair is long again, often falling to the shoulders, though most figures are still clean shaven. After 1550 the moustaches and beards return, though the hair is cut short again. Late Stuart brasses show great moustaches and rolling curls.

Women's hair is usually obscured by the headdress. Unmarried girls, such as Joan Plessi (c.1360) at Quainton, Bucks. (Fig. 101), are shown with streaming hair, while a few married women, Joan, Lady Cromwell at Tattershall (Fig. 92) being one, also follow this fashion. A remarkable creation is displayed by Margaret Chute (1614) at Marden, Hereford., whose hair (which must have been supported on wires) is brushed up to a lace crown.

Certain professional men and royal officers wear distinctive dress. The legal profession is especially important and well represented. Barons of the Exchequer and justices are generally shown wearing a coif, a sleeved gown, a fur tippet, a mantle buttoned on the right shoulder and a hood. John Cottusmore (1439), Chief Justice of the Common Pleas, at Brightwell Baldwin, Oxon., is typical (Fig. 51). John Martyn (1436) at Graveney, Kent, is a particularly fine example. The costume of the serjeants-at-law of the Bench of Common Pleas, from among whom many of the judges were chosen, is best illustrated by Thomas Rolf (1440) at Gosfield, Essex. He is dressed in a cassock-like gown, tabard and fur-

Fig. 44. Catherine D'Aut, her brother and a guardian angel, 1460. St Jacques, Bruges, Belgium. Length 77″. Flemish work.

Fig. 45. Thomas Pownder and wife, 1525. The Museum, Ipswich, Suffolk. Length 45½″. Originally at St Mary Quay church.

edged tippet and his coif alone distinguishes his robes from those used in the universities. Notaries are represented in normal civilian dress with a pen case and ink horn hanging from the girdle. St Mary Tower, Ipswich, has two excellent examples. A tall cap of velvet is worn by lawyers at Rodmarton, Glos., and St Peter's, Chester. The only surviving brass showing a herald is that of Robert Longe (1620) at Broughton Gifford, Wilts.. The herald wearing a tabard of arms appears incidentally in an allegorical design. There are three brasses to Yeomen of the Guard displaying the badge of the Rose and Crown on their doublets. One of them, Thomas Mountagu (1630) at Winkfield, Berks., is shown holding a halberd. The civic mantle, buttoned on the right shoulder, is worn by aldermen and mayors from 1430 onwards. Its form is identical to the mantle often shown on fourteenth-century figures, but it is often depicted thrown back over the left shoulder, exposing the fur lining. Richard Atkinson (1574) at St Peter in the East, Oxford, wears the mayor's scarf in addition to the mantle.

A few civilians, though dressed in the customary manner, carry unusual equipment. William Vynter (?) (1416) at Baldock, Herts., is represented with a hunting horn, rope, baselard and small hunting knives. Richard Bertlot (1462) at Stopham, Sussex, holds his staff of office as Marshal of the Hall to the Earl of Arundel. John Deynes (1527) at Beeston Regis, Norfolk, has a seaman's whistle slung round his neck. Thomas Cotes (1648) at Wing, Bucks., is shown with his keys, Cotes having been porter at Ascot Hall.

Children are often illustrated with their parents after 1420. Their dress is usually the same as the adults but in miniature. An exceptional case is the daughters of Sir Thomas Urswyk (1479) at Dagenham, Essex, where the six youngest wear a form of the steeple headdress (Fig. 52). There is no other representation of this conical arrangement on brasses. Independent figures of children, usually representing them in skirted dresses, occur at the close of the sixteenth century. Freiberg in Germany has several examples where the children stand in thin dresses holding candles. Two seventeenth-century brasses at St George's Chapel, Windsor, are very unusual; they show the children of Dr John King in their cradles. Both died in infancy.

It is appropriate to end this section with foot supports, many of which relate to the person commemorated.

The most usual form of support for the feet are plots of earth or animals. Most knights before 1520 are shown

Fig. 46. Richard Wakehurst and wife, 1500. Ardingly, Sussex. Length 56".

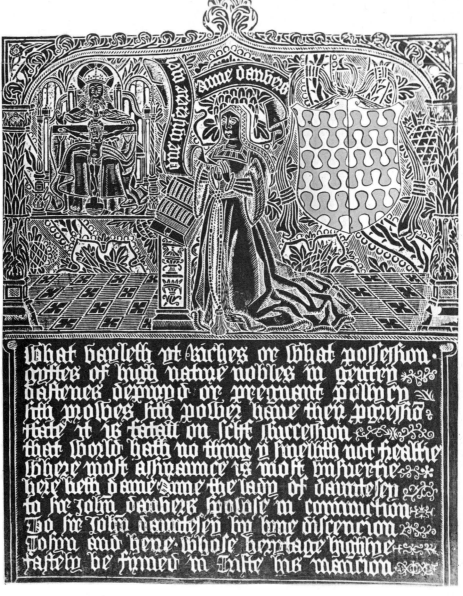

Fig. 47. Anne Danvers, 1539. Dauntsey, Wilts. Length 20½″. Rubbing by H. F. Owen Evans.

resting their feet on lions or hounds, while small dogs play in the folds of the wives' dresses. There are, however, two cases of pet dogs being identified: 'Terri' below the feet of Alice Cassy at Deerhurst, Glos., and 'Jakke' formerly at the feet of Sir Brian de Stapilton at Ingham, Norfolk.

Many foot supports have heraldic relevance, such as the bear of the Beauchamps at Warwick (1406), the unicorn of the Chaucers at Ewelme, Oxon. (1436), the whelk shell of the Wylloughbys at Wollaton, Notts. (1471), and most spectacular, the elephant and 'castle' of the Beaumonts

Fig. 48. Ralph Hawtrey and wife, 1574. Ruislip, London. Length 21″.

at Wivenhoe, Essex (1507) (Fig. 53). A few supports have
a reference to the name of the deceased. The dragon of
St Margaret appears from the folds at the feet of Margaret Wylloughby (1483) at Raveningham, Norfolk. Many
supports are purely decorative, as the Wyverns and
hairy wild men shown at the feet of Flemish prelates
and merchants. The variety of animals used is remarkable, and includes the stag, the bull, the horse, the squir-
rel and even a hedgehog.
A few continental examples refer to the history of the
deceased. St Henry at Nausis presses his murderer, Lalli,

Fig. 49. Duchess Sybella Elizabeth, 1606. Freiberg, Saxony, East Germany. Length about 100″. German work engraved in the Hilliger foundry. Illustration from Gerlach.

Fig. 50. The daughters of Sir Edward Filmer, 1629. East Sutton, Kent. Detail. Engraved by Edward Marshall.

underfoot, while two bishops at Paderborn, Germany, rest their feet on knights believed to represent the enemies of the diocese (Fig. 63).

A most interesting series of foot-rests indicate the trade of the deceased. The export of wool formed England's most lucrative trade in the fourteenth, fifteenth and sixteenth centuries. The organisation of this trade was based on the staple, or market, of Calais, and on the Company of the staple, a highly privileged guild of merchants which controlled the marketing and transport of wool. Several guild members are commemorated on

Fig. 52. The daughters of Sir Thomas Urswyk, 1479. Dagenham, Essex. Detail.

brasses and the merchants of the Gloucestershire Cotswolds and Lincolnshire Wolds are particularly well represented. Their brasses are among the finest of the fifteenth century.

The exceptional feature of these monuments is the arrangement of rams, sheep, and wool sacks below the feet of the figures (Figs. 56, 57). Northleach, Glos., has the largest and most varied collection. A woolman and wife of c. 1400 and John Fortey (1458) are particularly fine. Small flocks of sheep resting under trees are engraved in the pediment of the canopies of Thomas Bushe and wife (1526). Robert Page and wife (1440) at Cirencester, Glos., are commemorated by a large canopied brass. The woolpack under Robert's feet is engraved with a shield and merchant's mark. The most important Lincolnshire examples are at Lynwode and All Saints, Stamford, to the families of Lyndewode and Browne, all of whom stand on woolpacks. The most splendid brass to a wool merchant is that of William Grevel and wife (1401) at Chipping Camden, but they have no special foot-rest (Fig. 39).

Other trades are represented. Two vinters at Cirencester, Glos. (Fig. 58), and Barton on the Humber, Lincs., rest on wine casks. William Scors (1447), a tailor, at Northleach, has shears at his feet (Fig. 59). A reused fragment at Lambourne, Essex, shows a fold of linen at

Fig. 53. Elephant and castle and broomcod at the feet of William, Viscount Beaumont, 1507. Wivenhoe, Essex. Detail.

the feet of a clothier (?). Foot-rests are a rewarding study justifying a specialist interest.

4. *Ecclesiastical figures*

The clergy formed a very influential body in medieval society and about six hundred figure brasses represent secular clerics, members of the universities and the monastic orders. The minor orders of secular clergy, doorkeepers, exorcists, lectors and acolytes, are not represented as main figures, though acolytes and lectors bearing candles and books respectively are depicted as 'weepers' in the canopy of Bishop Novak (1452) at Wroclaw. The major orders, the deacons, priests and lords spiritual, are well represented, though the vestments of deacons are mostly illustrated on subsidiary figures on canopies. The form of church vestments was established throughout western Europe before the thirteenth century, and underwent only minor changes until the Protestant 'Reformation' of the sixteenth century. Even then the modifications are only represented on English brasses. The difference between a fourteenth-century brass of a priest in mass vestments and a fifteenth-century example

Fig. 54. Eagle at the feet of Countess Isabel of Essex, 1483. Little Easton, Essex. Detail.

lies in the treatment and detail of the figures and not in the form of the robes. Ecclesiastical brasses cannot be easily analysed according to period, and it is necessary to examine them according to the dignity of the deceased and the function of the vestments represented.

A distinctive feature of medieval male ecclesiastical figures is the tonsure, the shaving of the crown of the head. The tonsure on brasses is barely distinguishable from a skull cap, though the tonsure of John Rode (1470) at Bremen, Germany, is stippled to indicate stubble.

The robe worn by a priest for general use was the cassock, a long coat, buttoned down the front and usually black in colour. A priest (c.1480) at Cirencester, Glos., is represented in the cassock alone. Thomas Awmarle (1402) at Cardynham, Cornwall, wears it with a girdle, hood and baselard, providing a good illustration of outdoor dress (Fig. 61).

It is necessary to divide ceremonial vestments into two main groups — the eucharistic and the processional vestments.

(i) *Eucharistic or mass vestments*   The vast majority of

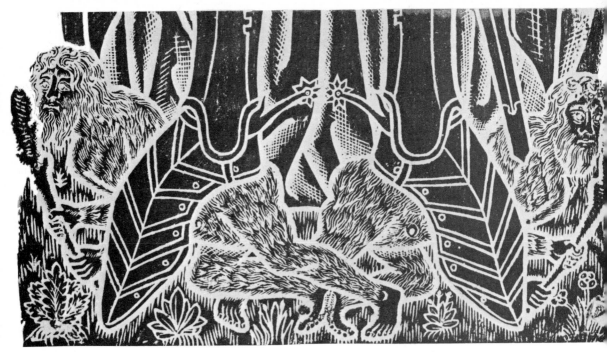

Fig. 55. Wildmen at the feet of Ralph, Baron Cromwell, c. 1470. Tattershall, Lincs. Detail.

Fig. 56. Woolpack at the feet of John Lyndewode the Younger, 1421. Linwood, Lincs. Detail.

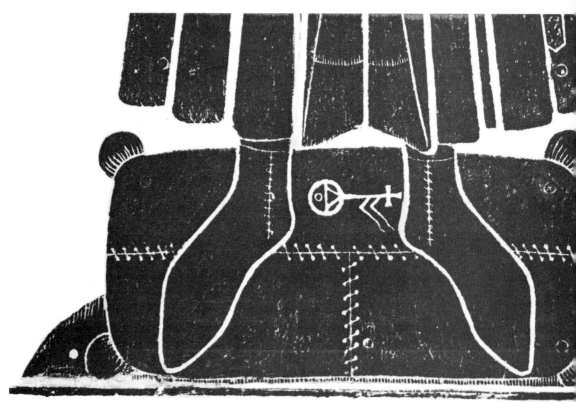

Fig. 57. Sheep and woolpack from the brass of an unknown woolman, c. 1485. Northleach, Glos. Detail.

Fig. 58. Wine cask at the feet of an unknown vintner, c. 1400. Cirencester, Glos. Detail.

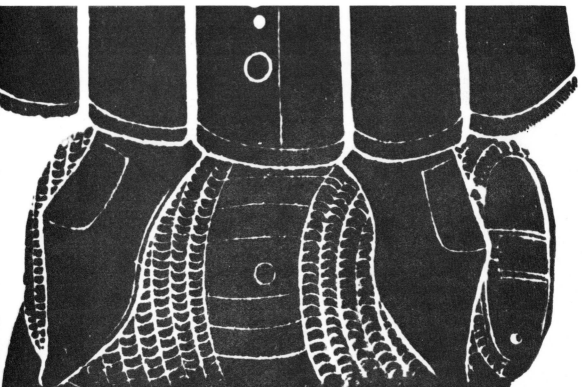

Fig. 59. Scissors at the feet of William Scors, a tailor, 1447. Northleach, Glos.
Detail.

ecclesiastical brasses show priests vested for mass and often holding the chalice and wafer of the Blessed Sacrament in their hands. The vestments themselves have their origin in Early Christian Church practice, and have acquired symbolic significance. The first vestment worn over the cassock is the amice, a hood of linen with an apparel, worn at the neck and tied by strings crossing at the priest's back. The second is the alb, a long robe of white linen reaching the feet and bound at the waist by a girdle or cord. It is decorated with six pieces of embroidery called apparels, which are usually visible at the cuffs and lower front hem. The apparels at the back hem and on the back and breast are concealed by other vestments. A long strip of embroidered silk, the stole, is hung round the neck, crossed over the breast and held in place by the cord of the alb. A similar but shorter vestment, the maniple, is worn over the left wrist. Over all is worn the chasuble, a fine vestment of silk or precious cloth frequently decorated with embroidered orphreys. The shape of the chasuble is almost circular, the priest's head passing through the centre. Excellent examples of priests so vested are at Higham Ferrers, Northants. (1337) (Fig. 60), Horsmonden, Kent (1340), Wensley, Yorks. (c. 1360) (Fig. 62), North Mimms, Herts.

ig. 61. Thomas Awmarle, c. 1400. Cardynham, Cornwall. Height of figure 14″.

3.60. Laurence de St Maur, 1337.
gham Ferrers, Northants. Length of fig-
e 63″. Rich canopy omitted.

(c.1360), Shottesbrooke, Berks. (1370), Northfleet, Kent (1375), Crondall, Hants. (1381), Edlesborough, Bucks. (1395), Great Bromley, Essex (1432), Bremen Cathedral (1470), Erfurt Cathedral, Germany (1422) and Hospice St Josse, Bruges (1584). Occasionally the stole or maniple are omitted, especially on brasses made in East Anglia and the Midlands. The form of the stole is best illustrated on the small figure of John West (1415) at Sudborough, Northants., who wears no chasuble.

Additional vestments worn by bishops and archbishops are well illustrated on brasses. These vestments consist of a jewelled double-peaked headdress, the mitre, a ring, jewelled silk gloves, embroidered sandals, buskins of embroidered silk, and the tunicle and the dalmatic, two richly ornamented vestments open at the sides, with fringed edges and cuffs. The dalmatic fringed on one or both sides was worn by deacons and is illustrated on subsidiary figures of St Stephen. The mitre is shown on thirteenth-century brasses as low and simple in form. Its grandeur and height increased in the following centuries and several of the fifteenth-century mitres depicted are exquisite. Many are enriched with crockets and jewelled orphreys. The mitre of the bishop Andreas at Poznan was embroidered with a representation of the Annunciation. Two lappets called infulae hang from the back of the mitre. These are usually indicated on brasses, and are sometimes brought forward on to the shoulders for decorative effect. Bishops are shown holding the pastoral staff with a curved volute called the crozier. A banner, the vexillum, usually hangs from the staff.

There are eleven brasses to bishops in England, all of which are good illustrations of these vestments. Brasses were widely used for episcopal memorials and it is unfortunate that this class has suffered particularly heavily, on account of the despoilation. The finest examples are at Hereford (1360), Adderley, Salop. (c.1390), and Ely Cathedral (1554). Among many continental examples those of Germany at Constance, Lübeck, Paderborn (Fig. 63), Schwerin and Zeitz, and of Spain at Avila, are particularly outstanding. Bishop Bowthe of Exeter (1478) at East Horsley, Surrey, is remarkable in showing the back of the chasuble as the bishop kneels in prayer.

Archbishops were entitled to wear the pall, a woollen vestment of Y shape, hanging both front and back with weighted ends, and decorated with crosses. A cross staff was carried before them. Brasses to archbishops are rare but usually elaborate. Robert de Waldeby (1397), Archbishop of York, at Westminster Abbey, and Thomas Cranley (1417), Archbishop of Dublin, at New College, Oxford, are particularly fine. William de Grenefeld (1315), Archbishop of York, at York Minster, is sadly mutilated. A small figure of an archbishop (c.1500) – probably intended to be St Thomas of Canterbury – taken down from the tower at Edenham, Lincs., presents the vestments very clearly. Archbishop Jakob of Siena at Gniezno wears no pall, but holds cross staff and crozier. A number of German bishops were entitled to wear the pall, especially those of the See of Bamberg.

The only brasses to cardinals, Nicholas of Cues (1488) at Cues, Germany, and Frederick, son of Cazimir, (1510) at Krakow, Poland (Fig. 84), present the deceased in mass vestments. Frederick is fully vested with the omission of the stole. Nicholas is vested in mitre, chasuble, amice, alb and gloves. The broad-brimmed cardinal's hat with its pendants is engraved above the shields represented. There are no brasses to popes, though a representation of Pope Gregory in mass vestments and tiara forms part of the 'mass of St Gregory' above the figure of Roger Legh (1506) at Macclesfield, Cheshire.

(ii) *Processional vestments* Processional vestments were generally used in great churches on ceremonial occasions other than the mass and are often illustrated

Fig. 62. Sir Simon de Wensley, c. 136 Wensley, Yorks. Length 66″. Flemish wo

on brasses of canons, deans and wardens. These vestments are the surplice, a loose white linen garment with wide sleeves, the almuce, a heavy fur hood with two long pendants in the front, and the cope, a semi-circular sleeveless mantle. These vestments are most commonly represented together, as on William Ermyn (1401) at Castle Ashby, Northants. (Fig. 64). The cope envelops and obscures the other vestments.

The cope originated as a practical garment, fastened across the breast with a clasp and provided with a hood to protect the wearer. This form is illustrated by the plain choral copes worn by ecclesiastics at Watton, Herts. (c.1370), and Cottingham, Yorks. (1383). A much more elaborate form of this vestment, the festive cope, is generally represented. This cope was made of precious cloth with embroidered orphreys and an elaborate clasp or morse. A decorative flap at the back took the place of the hood. Brasses to priests wearing these elaborate copes are among the finest in England. Especially good examples are at St Cross, Winchester, Hants. (1382), Fulbourne, Cambs. (1391), Balsham, Cambs. (1401 and 1462), Bottesford, Leics. (1404), Ringwood, Hants. (1416), Merton College, Oxford (1471), Tattershall, Lincs. (1510), and Trinity Hall, Cambridge (1517). Many of the orphreys are beautifully decorated with figures of saints and floral or geometric patterns. The initials of the names of ecclesiastics are worked into certain orphreys as at Broadwater, Sussex (1432), while at Warbleton, Sussex (1436), the orphrey is inscribed with the text from Job XIX, verses 25 and 26. The design of the morse is often intricate. At Castle Ashby and Fulbourne the morse is engraved with a shield of arms, at Knebworth, Herts., with the face of Christ, at Bottesford, Leics., with the Holy Trinity, and at Havant, Hants., with an initial. The word 'Jesus' or its contractions, as at Sessay, Yorks., is occasionally found. In a few examples the entire cope is embroidered, as on John Blodwell (1462) at Balsham and Robert Langton (1518) at the Queen's College, Oxford. William Langeton (1413) at Exeter Cathedral, Devon, is especially interesting in that his kneeling pose reveals the full form of the cope.

The finest brasses to coped priests are in England, though there are good figures at Zeitz and Erfurt in Germany and Amiens in France.

The almuce worn over the surplice but not concealed by the cope, is represented on a number of English and continental brasses. The surface of the brass is often cut away for lead inlay to simulate fur. The form of the almuce with its two pendants and fringe of tails is well shown on the figure of James Coorthopp (1557), Dean of Peterborough, at Christ Church Cathedral, Oxford (Fig. 65). Other fine English examples are at Manchester Cathedral (1458), Tredington, Worcs. (1482), Eton College, Bucks. (1503), and Burwell, Cambs. (c.1542). These vestments are beautifully represented in Germany at the cathedrals of Bamberg and Erfurt, and in Poland at Poznan. Hermann Schomekers (1406) at Bardowijk, Germany, wears the almuce over his head, and Hermann Wessel (1507) at Emden carries it over his right arm. Both arrangements are common on continental monuments.

A special privilege of the canons of St George's Chapel, Windsor, is to wear, as a processional vestment, the purple mantle of the Order of the Garter bearing a cross badge on the left shoulder. Roger Lupton (1540), Provost of Eton, at Eton College, is the best illustration.

The Religious Orders The power and influence of the monasteries throughout the Middle Ages was tremendous. The abbots, priors and monks are, however, poorly represented on brasses, thanks to the destruction and pillage of the monasteries during the sixteenth century. Two excellent brasses to abbots, Thomas de la Mare (c.1360) at St Alban's, Herts., and John Estney (1498) at Westminster Abbey, represent the figures in eucharistic vestments identical to those described for bishops. The Augustinian abbot, Richard Bewfforeste (c.1510) at Dorchester, Oxon., and John Norton (1509) at South Creake, Norfolk, bear the crozier. Both wear processional vestments, though Bewfforeste wears a monastic cloak and hood instead of the cope. More distinctive is the magnificent brass of Thomas Nelond (1433), Cluniac Prior of Lewes, at Cowfold, Sussex (Fig. 68). This shows the prior in the monastic habit of the Benedictine Order — the black cowl like a loose surplice with deep sleeves, and the hood attached to the scapula beneath. Similar habits are worn by Prior Langley (1437) of Horsham St Faith at St Lawrence, Norwich, and a group of monks at St Alban's. John Stodeley (1502) at Over Winchendon, Bucks., wears the white rochet, or tunic, and hooded cloak of the canons regular of St Augustine. A friar (c.1440) at Great Amwell, Herts., wears a tunic, a knotted cord and sandals (Fig. 67).

A few members of the female orders are represented, mainly nuns and vowesses, widows who took vows (Fig. 38). Their habit is similar to the costume of widows which has been described. Two abbesses at Elstow, Beds.

Fig. 64. William Ermyn, 1401. Castle Ash Northants. Length 64".

Fig. 65. Canon James Coorthopp, 1557. Christchurch, Oxford. Length 32".

Fig. 66. Richard Wyard, 1478. New College, Oxford. Length 30".

(c.1520), and Denham, Bucks. (1540), are likewise attir-
ed, the former bearing a crozier. The kneeling figure of
Abbess Scornay at Nivelles, Belgium, presents the same
habit in profile.

The Universities Some eighty clerics are represented
in academic dress. Their brasses mostly lie in the college chapels of Oxford and Cambridge. The great majority of these figures date from 1440 to 1550, though
John Hotham (1361) at Chinnor, Oxon., is one of the few
fourteenth-century examples. Most of the figures are of
modest size with the striking exceptions of the mutilated
figures of Eudo de la Zouch (c.1414) at St John's College
and John Holbrook (1436) at St Mary the Less, both at
Cambridge and both former Chancellors of the University.

It is difficult to discriminate between the academical
habits represented, as differences in colour are not recorded. All appear to have been worn over the cassock.
Doctors are probably distinguished by wearing a stiff
round cap, a sleeveless gown with a slit in front through
which the hands were passed and an academical hood.
The hood is well defined on the brass of Dr Richard Bil-
lingford (1442) at St Benet's, Cambridge, who is shown
in profile. Masters and Bachelors are shown in a variety
of habits comprising an academic gown and hood. Occasionally academic status is indicated by a scarf which is
held by a clasp to the left shoulder of the cassock.

A selection of academical figures can be studied in the
series of New College, All Souls College, Merton College
and Magdalen College, Oxford, and of King's College,
Cambridge (Fig. 66).

Brasses of academics after 1550 generally represent the
figures in normal civil dress, or with a gown and hood,
as at St John's College, Oxford.

An unusual brass which deserves special mention is Jacques Schelewaerts (1483), Doctor of Theology, at St Sauveur, Bruges, who is represented teaching in the University of Louvain (Fig. 69). The doctor is surrounded with
senior students at long desks, and accompanied by an
assistant with a staff.

Post Reformation Clergy in England The robes of the
Church of England prescribed by the first Prayer Book
of King Edward VI (1549) and upheld by Queen Elizabeth, are shown on several clerical brasses. The approv-
ed garments of the episcopate were the rochet, a modi-
fied form of alb of white linen, the chimere, a sleeveless
gown of black satin or silk, and a scarf. These robes are
worn by Bishop Geste (1578) at Salisbury Cathedral and

Fig. 67. A friar, c. 1440. Great Amwell
Herts. Length 16″.

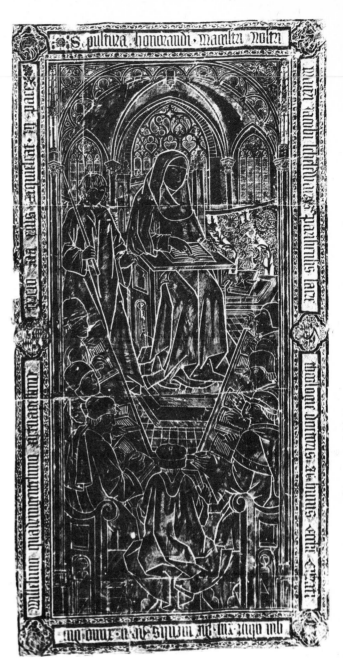

. 68. Prior Thomas Nelond, 1433. Cowfold.
sex. Length 123″. Illustration from Waller.

Fig. 69. Dr Jacob Schelewaerts, 1483. St Saveur,
Bruges, Belgium. Length 84″. Flemish work.

Bishop Robinson (1616) at Carlisle Cathedral and the Queen's College, Oxford. The rochet and chimere are worn in combination with a cope by Archbishop Harsnett (1631) at Chigwell, Essex.

Parish clergy are most usually represented in civil dress, but there are several brasses of clergy dressed in cassock, surplice and scarf, as William Dye (1567) at Westerham, Kent. Umphrey Tyndall (1614), Dean of Ely, at Ely Cathedral, dressed in a long gown with false sleeves and a scarf, is a fine example of the usual representation (Fig. 70).

5. *The Dead*

Commemoration of the deceased as dead persons in shrouds became very popular in the fifteenth century. The motive behind such representation was to illustrate the frailty of man. The injunction at the end of the inscription of John Brigge (1454) at Sall, Norfolk, is typical: 'As ye me se in soche degre so schall ye be a nothir day'. These sombre memorials could be dignified. The solemn peace of death is effectively portrayed in the heavily shrouded figures of Wouter Copman (1387) and Joris de Munter and wife (1439) at St Sauveur, Bruges. The realistic but gentle figures of the Palincks at Alkmaar, Holland (Fig. 71), are not offensive. Most shroud brasses are, however, less pleasing artistically, though effective in their message. The majority of English shroud brasses show an apparently living figure swathed in a shroud which is caught top and bottom into knots. Among many examples those at Sawbridgeworth, Herts. (1484), Cley, Norfolk (1512), and Loddon, Norfolk (1546), are particularly well executed.

A smaller group, cadavers and skeletons, are far more grotesque. These show the skeleton shrouded or bare, and bodies in a state of decomposition. Ralph Hamsterley (1510) at Oddington, Oxon. (Fig. 72), is represented as being devoured by worms, while the grinning skeletons at Aylsham, Norfolk (1507), and Hildersham, Cambs. (c.1530), are particularly ugly. Bishop Schönberg (1516) at Naumburg is hideously portrayed as standing before a rich curtain, his bowels dangling from his emaciated body.

Such compositions take unusual forms. At Lavenham, Suffolk, and Childrey, Berks., shrouded figures rise from their graves in answer to the last trump. A few sixteenth-century women who died in childbirth are represented lying in fourposter beds, the child resting on the coverlet. Anne Savage (1605) at Wormington, Glos., is an excellent brass in this design.

Fig. 70. Umphrey Tyndall D.D., 1614. Cathedral, Cambs. Length of figure 65"

71. Pieter Claessoen Palinck and wife, [1]6. Alkmaar, Holland. Length 96″. Illus-[ti]on from Creeny.

Fig. 72. Ralph Hamsterley, c. 1510. Oddington, Oxon. Length of figure 29½″. Foot inscription omitted.

Children who died in their first month, before their mothers' service of thanksgiving, are shown in their swaddling or chrysom bands. Elyn Bray (1516) at Stoke d'Abernon, Surrey (Fig. 73), is a perfect example. Anne Asteley (1512) at Blickling, Norfolk, holds two such chrysoms in her arms.

6. *Ancestral brasses*

There are a few brasses which set out to commemorate several generations of a family and show the deceased in line or in tiers. The most elaborate of such plates is that of Thomas Beale (1593) at Maidstone, Kent. Kneeling in six tiers are Thomas Beale, William of 1534, Robert of 1490, John of 1461, William of 1429 and John of 1399, all with their families and children. A smaller array to the Disney family is found at Norton Disney, Lincs., and three generations of Blondevilles kneel in line at Newton Flotman, Norfolk. Three ancestors of Stanislaus Czarnkowski (1602) at Czarnkow, Poland, make a naïve group with banners, swords and a mace. Such brasses were erected out of family pride and occur towards the close of the sixteenth century.

This description of the commemorated has covered a wide field, touching many sections of society, from royalty, dukes and cardinals, to the small farmer and trader and the parish priest. A brief analysis of costume and fashion has followed the description at every stage. The value of brasses as a social record should be clear, though very little reference has been made to the historical content of the inscriptions. These give much personal detail and provide a further valuable source for research. Nevertheless the matters described are only an aspect of the study. Brasses should be examined not only for what they portray, but for what they are.

Fig. 73. Elyn Bray, 1516. Stoke D'Abernon, Surrey. Length of figure 12″.

NICOLAO THOMICZKI VEXILLI
FERO POSNANIENSI PACE ET BELLO
CLARO AC SINGVLARI VIRTVTE PRVDE
CIA PIETATE VITE INNOCENCIA ETCVL
TV DEI AC RELIGIONIS INSIGNI PE.
TRVS CRACOVIENSIS ET POSNANI
ENSIS EPISCOPVS ET REGNI POLO
NIE VICECANCELLARIVS PARENTI
OPTIMO AC BENEMERENTI POSVITDIE
SECVNDA MENSISIVLY M·D·XXIIII:

Fig. 74. Nicholas Tomiczki, 1524. Ensign of Poznan. Tomice, Poland. Length 108″. Probably made in Cracow. Classical detail engraved in borders and background.

3 THE WORKSHOPS AND ENGRAVERS

The origin and age of brasses cannot be assessed nor their quality fully appreciated, without an understanding of the conditions under which they were made. The identity of the engravers and the location and organisation of their workshops, are matters requiring much future research, and this chapter is no more than a summary of facts and ideas so far obtained on these important subjects. The following are the main aspects of the engraver's work.

1. *The Agreement*

Brasses were made according to a contract between the engraver and the customer. Four different classes of customers can be defined. The first were men who sought their own memorial in their lifetime. Of such was Bishop Andreas of Bnin, at Poznan, Poland, whose brass was made twenty years before his death to satisfy his morbid contemplation. The second were civil or ecclesiastical bodies who were interested in the commemoration of their members, founders or heroes. The agreement of the Gniezno Chapter with a Wroclaw engraver, Tawchen, in 1462, for the brass of Archbishop Sprowa, is an example of this interest; while the brass to St Ethelred, King of the West Saxons, at Wimborne, Dorset, is most probably another (Fig. 75). The third class were executors of wills in which directions were left for the laying of brasses. The wills of John de Foxley of Bray (1378), of John Annsell, Merchant Taylor of London (1516), and Samuel Harsnett, Archbishop of York (1630) give very clear directions. The fourth class were descendants and relatives of the deceased, who wished to erect a monument for reasons of affection, pride or duty.

The difference between these classes of customers had an important influence. While the third and fourth classes generally ensured that the brass was made shortly after the death of the commemorated, the first and second arranged its making long before or after. For this reason the date on the inscriptions usually, but not always, approximates to the date of engraving. The age of brasses of foreign import, or those representing founders or benefactors, are however suspect, and their style of engraving should be examined closely. Incomplete inscriptions, as that of Thomas de la Mare at St Albans, Hertfordshire, the omission of dates on inscriptions, as on that of John Yong (1526), New College, Oxford, or the completion of the date by a different hand, are all indications of engraving in the deceased's

Fig. 75. St Ethelred, King of the West Saxons, d. 871. Inscribed 873 in error. Engraved c. 1440. Wimborne Minster, Dorset. Length of figure 14".

76. Anthony Darcy, 1540. Tolleshunt cy, Essex. Length 48″. Designed in ation of an early fifteenth-century fig-

lifetime. An extreme case is that of John de Cobham, at Cobham, who died in 1407 but whose brass, judging from its style, cannot have been engraved later than 1370 (Fig. 20). Significantly he is shown holding a model of the college he founded. Brasses laid long after decease are detectable by their incongruity of style, as Richard Wakehurst and wife at Ardingly, Sussex. They died in 1454 and 1464 respectively, but their brass is clearly no earlier than 1500 (Fig. 46).

The few actual agreements which can be traced contain detailed specifications. A contract of 1311 for the brass of a canon of Tournai involving Master Jaques Couvès describes the design and colour inlay. The agreement with Tawchen already mentioned specifies the form and dress of the figure, the nature and placing of the heraldic arms, the inlay of the shields with a silver mix, the precise joining of plates and the date for completion. A German account of 1643 with Hans Willhelm Hilliger of Freiberg, lays down the consistency of the metal, the polishing of the surface and the inlay of the engraving with black colour. John Annsell's will specifies the exact wording of the inscription, and representations of the Agnus Dei and pelican above the figures.

A particularly interesting clause of the Wroclaw contract required Tawchen to base his design on an earlier brass at Gniezno to Archbishop Jastrzambiec. Jastrzambiec, according to his own recorded statment to the Gniezno Chapter in 1422, had himself already ordered his brass from Bruges, to be based on the model of a fourteenth-century brass at Gniezno. These directions to follow earlier examples must have ensured a curious conservatism in design, and fully explains the persistence of old forms and antiquated conventions in many compositions. Some of the copies are remarkable. The border of John Clingenberg (1356), formerly at St Peter's, Lübeck, is reproduced exactly on the brass of John Lüneborch (1474) at St Catherine's, Lübeck (Fig. 110). At Poznan, the Flemish brass of Bishop Andreas clearly acted as a model for the architectural detail of the brasses made at Nuremberg for the Gorka family. Fourteenth-century Flemish style continued to be used well into the fifteenth century by Flemish, German and Silesian engravers. Certain English brasses are blatant copies of earlier work; Peter Rede (1568) at St Peter, Mancroft, Norwich, is a reproduction of a figure of 1470, while Anthony Darcy (1540) at Tolleshunt Darcy, Essex, is based on a model of 1420 (Fig. 76). The kneeling figures of Nicholas Garneys and family (c.1595) at

Fig. 77. Interior of a brass foundry from the treatise of Ercker. B marks the furnace in action, C the arrangment of crucibles and G the stone mould. Illustration from Monumental Brass Society transactions.

Fig. 78. Canon Heinrich Gassman, 1481. Erfurt Cathedral, Germany. Incised slab with brass inlays. Length of head 16".

Ringsfield, Suffolk, are copies from those of John Garneys and family (1524) at Kenton, Suffolk, made clearly on the order of Nicholas.

2. Manufacture

The task of completing the order lay with the engraver. He had to cast or obtain the plate, make or acquire designs, engrave the brass and deliver it complete with slab to its destination.

Medieval and Renaissance brass plate differed from modern brass in both consistency and manufacture. It was calamine brass, formed through the permeation of copper by zinc vapour derived from calamine ore. Details of the casting process are known from the sixteenth-century Italian and German authorities, Biringuccio and Ercker. Lumps of copper and calamine ore were placed together in crucibles and heated. The brass when liquid was poured into larger crucibles and from them into stone moulds (Fig. 77). The cast plate could be used as it was, or hammered into thinner sheet. The

gs. 79, 80. Details of Fig. 78.

beating of brass plate with water-driven hammers to produce thin sheet was known as the process of battery. The hammer marks are easily discernible on the back of Elizabethan English brass. Poor casting is revealed by a pitted plate surface or by the insertion of small pieces of brass to eradicate flaws. The plate itself was generally called 'latton', translated into Latin as *auricalcum*, the gold copper. Chemical analysis carried out on a dozen specimens has shown their plate to contain about 75% copper, 20% zinc and small quantities of lead and iron. The variation in the copper content ranged from 64% to 79%. Large plates were difficult to cast, and all sizeable brasses are made up of a number of pieces.

The engravers did not necessarily cast their own plate. The factors governing the location of engraving centres were those of commerce and transport, rather than immediate access to raw materials. Until the sixteenth century the English engravers had no adequate local source of materials. Practically all brass plate was imported from Flanders, France or Cologne, Cullen (Cologne) plate being specifically ordered for the latton tomb of Richard Beauchamp at St Mary, Warwick. Probably Flanders rather than Germany was the main source of supply. England's need for imported latton was resolved by the incorporation in 1568 of the Mines Royal and the Mineral and Battery Works, joint stock companies established for the production of plate. Even in Flanders itself the engravers concentrated in the west round Bruges, while the main copper deposits were in the Ardennes.

Latton plate could be worked and decorated in a number of ways. The sheet could be engraved in its entirety. Alternatively figures, inscriptions and details could be accurately cut out for separate inlay, and small features such as faces, hands and chalices could be cut to enrich incised slabs or sculptured figures. These techniques were not the prerogative of any particular workshop. While rectangular sheet compositions are common on the continent, a large number of Flemish, German and Silesian brasses are of separate inlay. Many late sixteenth-century English brasses are on rectangular sheet, although economy of metal favoured the use of separate inlay in England before 1570. The inlay of small details is met widely on the continent and is well illustrated by the slab of Heinrich Gassman (1481) at Erfurt Cathedral (Figs. 78-80). Much engraved latton enriches the tombs of King Richard II and King Edward III at Westminster Abbey. Conversely stone or alabaster details were incorporated into brasses. According to old rubbings, the head of John Yong at New College, Oxford, was of composition, while the inlaid face of Queen Ingeborg at Ringstead still remains.

The engraving tool, the burin, was quadrangular in section and its edges could be used for broad as well as fine cutting. The engraving could be varied to produce special effects. Usually the design was incised, but in some cases the surface was cut away leaving the lines or lettering in flat relief. Katherine Scrop (1500) at Hambledon, Bucks., is a beautiful example of this treatment (Fig. 81). The technique of semi-relief, in which lines were not clean cut but worked into shallow sculptured forms, was popular in Silesia. Archbishop Jakob of Siena (1480) at Gniezno (Fig. 87) is an example, though rubbings cannot adequately reproduce the full quality of this form. The only English instance known to the author is the reused fragment of a deacon at Burwell, Cambs. Semi-relief should not be confused with low relief casting, in which the surface of the plate is moulded, which was very popular in Germany.

Colour could also be added as decoration. The lines of most brasses were inlaid with black mastic; others were filled with coloured wax and resins. Heraldic dresses and shields were often inlaid, and traces of colour can usually be detected with a magnifying glass in the hatched surfaces. The Earl of Essex and his Countess (1483) at Little Easton, Essex, still retain much of this inlay. Lead, often inserted to simulate silver, is used extensively on the kirtle of Alice Shelton (1424) at Great Snoring, Norfolk, and on the kirtle and mantle of Elizabeth Fynderne (1444) at Childrey, Berks. Enamelling was a rare and expensive form of decoration. The splendid blue shield of Sir John d'Abernon and the heraldic tabard and mantle of John Say and wife (1473) at Broxbourne, Herts., are two English examples. In exceptional cases the slab bore a colourful background. The fragments of the brass to John de Valence (1277) at Westminster Abbey are set in glass mosaic, and there are traces of a similar treatment to Sir Hugh Hastings (1347) at Elsing, Norfolk.

The designs of brasses were based on drawings, which were derived from a number of sources. English engravers in the sixteenth century apparently made their own. The sketches by Gerard Johnson of Southwark of the Gage brasses at West Firle, Sussex, are still preserved, and the correspondence connected with them reflects a close liaison between Johnson and John Gage. Alternatively engravers turned to local artists to produce draw-

Fig. 81. Katherine Scrop, widow, 15 Hambledon, Bucks. Length of figure 9'

Fig. 82. Confused engraving on the br of Richard Chernok, c. 1490. Shapw Dorset. Detail.

83. Dürer woodcut of Nicholas Ulrich Erasmus from which the side figures of 84 were copied.

Fig. 84. Cardinal Frederick, 1510. Cracow Cathedral, Poland. Length 112″. Engraved by Hermann Vischer the Younger.

ings. While the Nowemiasto brass seems to have been designed by Master Peter of the Marienberg, court painter to the Teutonic Order, the casting and metal work was undertaken by Ludwison of Bremen. The Hilliger family of Freiberg worked in conjunction with Dresden artists, in particular Andreas Götting, whose initials appear on some of the brasses. Other engravers copied existing drawings and pictures. Hermann Vischer the Younger of Nuremberg used Dürer woodcuts as models, and the relationship between the figures of Saints Albert and Stanislaus on the brass of Cardinal Frederick of Krakow, and Saints Nicholas and Erasmus on the Dürer woodcut is obvious (Figs 83, 84). The great brass at Freiberg to Henry the Pious, Duke of Saxony (1541) by another engraver, is a clear copy of the duke's portrait by Lucas Cranach. Other famous artists whose style has been identified on brasses are Berndt Knotke and Veit Stoss. The practice of copying on order has been described, and these copies must have involved the work of a local artist or brass rubber. It would be interesting to know how the pattern of the Italian incised slab to Cardinal Nicholas of Cues at St Peter ad Vincula, Rome, reached Aachen or Cologne, to be used again, though adapted, for the cardinal's brass at Cues.

Occasionally the design was not properly carried out or economies had to be made. Meaningless lines and errors are found on some of the greatest brasses. The detail from Gniezno reveals a number of lightly-cut guide lines curving beyond their proper limit (Fig. 87). The Chartham and Trumpington knights are both unfinished (Figs 17,15). On the former the mail links have only been completed on the right foot, while on the latter the ground of the shield has been partially cut away. Richard Chernok, priest (c.1490) at Shapwick, Dorset, is a curious case. The scarf over his cassock seems to have been forgotten and had subsequently to be imposed over a rosary and bag (Fig. 82).

When the engraving was complete the brass was set into the stone. An indent was first cut into the stone, so that the metal could lie flush with the surface. Recesses were made in the indent to receive lead plugs. Flanged brass rivets were set into these. The indent was then flooded with pitch. The brass, into which appropriate rivet holes had been drilled, was then lowered on to the rivets. The rivet tops were hammered out and rubbed flush with the surface with a water stone. On certain brasses the rivet tops have been engraved to give an imperceptible finish. Apparently the earliest brasses, for example at Lubiaz and Stoke d'Abernon, had no rivets and relied on the adhesive quality of the pitch. Occasionally brasses on table tombs were riveted into wooden plugs, which survive almost intact in an indent at Blythburgh, Suffolk. Others were strengthened with reinforcing bars, which locked into a deeper indent.

The great weight of the completed monument made water transport desirable. The monumental mason's misery with overland carriage, mire and broken axles is fully recorded in Gerard Johnson's travels to Bottesford in Leicestershire with the Rutland tombs.

3. The Cost

The cost of several brasses is known, but the information is too scattered and unrelated to be enlightening. The brasses and stone of Sir John de St Quintin and wife (1397) at Brandsburton, Yorks., cost twenty marks. The

Figs. 85-86. Sir John de Creke and wi c. 1325. Westley Waterless, Cambs. An graver's mark is at the left-hand base c ner of the lady's brass. Length of kni 66". Rubbing by R. Greenwood.

much smaller brass of Sir John Curson at Bylaugh, Norfolk, cost eight marks in 1471. The modest brass of Robert Gosebourne (1523) at St Alphege, Canterbury, cost £4 10s. Continental records in Dutch guilders and Hungarian florins are even more obscure.

Scottish evidence of the import of Flemish brasses is more useful. The account of the brass to Duncan Liddel (1613) at the old church of Aberdeen has been preserved. This records that the metal cost £31 0s 6d, the engraving £53 with an additional bounty of salmon worth £3 and the expense of customs, transport, etc., £37 15s. Further valuable details are given in the ledger of Andrew Halyburton, Scottish 'consul' at Veere, near Middleburg, who undertook trading agencies. The brass or incised slab of James Stewart, Duke of Ross and Archbishop of St Andrews, cost £25, the pattern £1 8s, and packing and travel expenses from Bruges to Veere only a further £5 0s 2d. These figures are in Flemish currency and show that about one third of the expense of such imported brasses was spent on transport costs. The overall cost was substantial.

4. *The Workshops*

The location of the workshops where brasses were made and the identity of the engravers can be partially established by documentary evidence and also by the clear relationship of brasses in certain regions. Foundries were generally family businesses, handed on for several generations. The family tradition was reinforced by the guilds who, for example in Nuremberg, made many concessions to the sons of masters to encourage the craft. These well-established workshops had their own recognizable style.

In addition other distinctive qualities can be recognized in brasses engraved within a region. These qualities arose from fashions and artistic conventions established by the contact of local craftsmen. It is rarely possible to identify a particular workshop unless a brass is marked or signed. It is easier to recognize the characteristics of a group of workshops. The term 'school' is applied to brasses showing these group characteristics, whether issuing from one or a number of related centres. The most important schools were those of Bruges, London, Nuremberg and Paris.

The school of Bruges consisted of a number of workshops in west Flanders, clustered around Bruges, Ghent and Tournai. The dark bluish stone associated with this school was quarried near Tournai. The glory of the Bruges school is the superb, rectangular, sheet plate compositions of the fourteenth century, displaying

Fig. 87. Detail of Archbishop Jakob of Sie␣ 1480. Gniezno, Poland.

bishops or merchants lying beneath rich canopies filled with apostles, weepers, angels and representations of the Deity. The style is distinctive, especially its bold monumental figures with recessed lips and staring eyes, its abundance of tabernacles, and its exotic backgrounds. The greatest of these compositions, often classed as the most impressive brasses existing, are at Ringstead, Denmark (1319) (Fig.12), Schwerin (1347 and 1375) (Figs.88-94-5), Stralsund (1357) and Lübeck, Germany (1350), Torun, Poland (1361), and at King's Lynn (1349 and 1364), St Albans (c.1360) and Newark, England (1361).

The origin of these great brasses has been disputed, and some authorities have argued that they came from Lübeck not Bruges. It is now clear, however, that they came from Bruges. These brasses have a place in the development of Flemish engraving, but are alien to known north German work. They are comparable in style to Flemish incised slabs. Their distribution strongly favours Bruges when account is taken of all recorded evidence. All documentary evidence points to Flanders. The fourteenth-century wills of the Lübeck councillors, Wedekin Warendorp and Herman Gallin, ordered brasses of Flemish make. The Polish bishop Jastrzambiec stated in the Gniezno Chapter of 1426 that his own brass was being prepared in Bruges. The contract of 1311 with Master Jaques Couvès specifies a design similar to the brasses in question.

The tremendous output of the Bruges school can only be appreciated from the indents of the churches of Bruges and Ghent, from the scores of reused fragments in England (discussed in Chapter 5) and from the published drawings published by J. Gaillard. Flemish trade in brasses, from Italy in the south to Finland in the north, is proof of a European reputation.

London was undoubtedly the foremost English centre, responsible for about 75% of the existing English figure

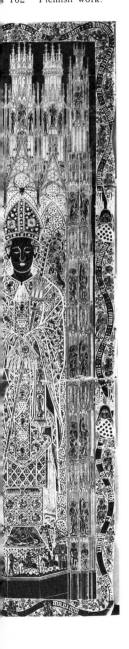

8. Bishops Godfrey and Frederick Bülow, 1375. Schwerin, Germany. Total 162" Flemish work.

brasses. London's importance is indicated by the distribution of brasses of similar style from Cumberland to Cornwall. The existence of large central workshops is confirmed by the study of reused fragments which show, for instance, that brasses at Walkern, Herts., Lee, Kent, Marsworth, Bucks., and Whichford, Warwick, were all cut from the same original. A number of sixteenth and seventeenth-century engravers have been identified. Several, Nicholas Stone and Francis Griggs, for example, were outstanding London sculptors. Gerard Johnson of Southwark has been mentioned. The brass of Edward Bulstrode (1599) at Upton, Bucks., is certainly from his workshop, as are four brasses to the Gage family at West Firle. Edward Marshall, king's master mason, signed the excellent Filmer brass (1629) at East Sutton, Kent. The remarkable sculptor Epiphany Evesham signed the brass to Edmund West (1618) at Marsworth, Bucks.

Of earlier London engravers, little can be certainly established. The Creke brass (c. 1325) at Westley Waterless, Cambs., bears a mark, an N, a star and a mallet, which has been associated with the seal of Walter le Mason (Figs 85, 86). The N occurs again on the Camoys brass (1419) at Trotton, Sussex, and may be a London guild mark. There is every reason to believe that the London marblers and lattoners who cast metal tombs were also engaged in brass engraving. Henry Yelverley, Stephen Lote, Nicholas Broker and Godfrey Prest were the marblers and coppersmiths responsible for the tomb of King Richard II. William Austen, founder, and Thomas Stevyns, coppersmith, were the craftsmen contracted for the metalwork on the tomb of Richard Beauchamp, Earl of Warwick, in 1449. The will of Thomas Salter, chantry priest, directed in 1558 that his figure should be 'graven in copper of a cunynge m(ar)bler that dwelleth in Sancte Dunstons p(ar)ishe in the west agaynste the south syde of the churche'. This brass unfortunately no longer exists and the marbler is unidentified. Christine Phelip, whose peculiar but fine brass of 1470 is at Herne, Kent, was the wife of Sir Matthew Phelip, a London goldsmith, and her brass was possibly engraved in her husband's workshop.

London work had no rigid conventions, unlike that of Bruges. Widely distributed English brasses of similar pattern, peculiarities and scripts can be confidently ascribed to the London workshops. Provincial schools can be located by the concentration of unusual work round a particular centre. The quality of London brasses varied with the workshop. A most curious group of ornamental but ill balanced knights was produced between 1350 and 1370, of which Sir John de Cobham (c.1365) is one. In contrast, a small group of brasses between the years 1540 and 1556, of which those to the Fermer family at Easton Neston, Northants., and Somerton, Oxon., are good examples, reveal a surprising excellence of engraving in a period of declining standards. The main sources of stone for the London craftsmen were the quarries of Purbeck, Dorset, Petworth, Sussex,. and Bethersden, Kent.

Nuremberg was the most celebrated German centre, reaching its greatest fame through the genius of the Vischer family. Herman Vischer the Elder, Peter the Elder and his grandson, Hermann, manufactured between 1460 and 1530 a great series of cast bronze tombs, mostly in relief but some in semi-relief or engraving. The greatest Vischer brasses are those up until 1520 to the ducal house of Saxony at Meissen, to the Gorka family at Poznan and Cardinal Casimir at Krakow. Canon Georg von Lewenstein (1464) at Bamberg Cathedral bears the family mark and a punning fish. As a collection they form the finest group of brasses from late German Gothic to the early German Renaissance. An earlier engraver working in or near Nuremberg, using the mark Z, made a number of brasses at Zeitz, Naumburg and Meissen between 1460 and 1480, similar, but inferior to, the early Vischer plates. The eminence of Nuremberg in this field of craftsmanship lasted from 1450 to 1550.

The obliteration of French brasses during the Revolution has been partly compensated by the series of drawings made by François-Roger de Gaignières which was presented to King Louis XIV of France in 1711. It is clear from these that Paris was a major and early centre of engraving, its products being similar but less intricate than those of Bruges. 'Guillaume de Plalli me fecit' is inscribed on the drawing of a thirteenth-century brass at Evreux.

There were other flourishing centres in addition to these four. In Flanders, Liége and Malines were particularly important, the former responsible for the great brass to the Heere brothers (1398) at Brussels Musées Royaux, and the latter for Abbot Betten (1607) whose coloured brass in the Museum de Bijloke, Ghent, is signed by Libert van Egheem of Malines. Of other centres in Germany, Aachen and Cologne were particularly productive in the fifteenth and sixteenth centuries. William Leomanz of Cologne, according to the *Annales Novimagi*, made the elaborate brass to Catherine de Bourbon at

Fig. 89. William, Baron Willoughby d'Ereby, and wife, c. 1410. Spilsby, Lincs. Leng of male figure 47".

74

90. Robert Brasyer, bellfounder, en-
ed c. 1513. St Stephen, Norwich, Nor-
. Length 28″. Wife and inscription
ted.

Nymwegen, Holland. The Baltic city ports were rich in metalworkers, Lübeck being outstanding, though their products, judged by Bishop Cremon (1377) at Lübeck and Queen Agnes (1432) at Gadebusch, were more grandiose than beautiful. The brass of Matteus Rodde (1677) at the Marienkirche is signed by the local founder, Wolfgang Hartmann. The capital of Silesia was a particularly interesting centre judging by the early separate inlay brasses in Lubiaz (Fig. 13) and The Cross Church, Wroclaw, and the fifteenth-century episcopal brasses in Wroclaw Cathedral. Jodocus Tawchen is the only known famous engraver of this city. Krakow was an important Polish city where the foundry of a Master Hanusz made brasses in the sixteenth century, possibly including the Tomice brass of 1524.

English provincial centres are particularly interesting and easily recognised. York and probably Stamford or Boston produced brasses of a very different style from those of London, and these are found concentrated in Yorkshire and Lincolnshire. William Willoughby d'Eresby (c.1410) at Spilsby, Lincs., is a fine early example (Fig. 89), and William Fitzwilliam (1474) at Sprotborough, Yorks., is a typical example of the fifteenth-century style. One of the peculiarities of fifteenth-century York brasses is the slimness of the knights, emphasized by their deep sallets and their long down-turned sabbotons. Lions are often shown staring upwards. Their ladies are simple in presentation. During the fifteenth century a number of brasses representing chalices were laid, and in the late sixteenth century a series of large half-effigies of unusual style was engraved. Robert Askwith (1597), mayor, from St Crux, York, is an example of the latter.

Norwich in the east probably surpassed York, but copied earlier York conventions, especially in the engraving of chalices. The period of greatest activity in the Norwich school was between 1430 and 1550. The family of Brasyer owned a large foundry in Norwich and was famous for bell casting. Robert, who died in 1435, his son Richard and grandson, Richard, were all civic dignatories and metalworkers, the grandson being also a goldsmith. Their brasses, which lie in St Stephen's, Norwich, are engraved in an unusual style (Fig. 90). The hands are held apart and forwards in an early Christian attitude of prayer, a pose which was often portrayed by the Norwich engravers. It is most probable that these brasses were made in the Brasyer foundry. East Anglian brasses are easily distinguishable by their rich but usually naive representation. Joan, Lady Cromwell (c.1475) at Tattershall, Lincs., is the finest example remaining of the school (Fig. 92). The treatment of her drapery, her hands and face are typical of the best Norwich work. The saints in the canopy shafts are very similar to Norfolk screen panel paintings, and the inclusion of St Edmund, king of East Anglia, is significant. The script of her inscription is identical to scores in Norfolk. Sir Roger le Strange (1506) at Hunstanton, Norfolk, is even more elaborate, with a triple canopy, side shafts with weepers and a bracket supporting the figure. The churches of Norwich are very rich in smaller but similar brasses, especially St John Maddermarket. Chalices, usually shown against a hatched background, were commonly used for priests' memorials, while small inscriptions were laid in remarkable numbers. Norwich brasses have their main concentration in Norfolk and Suffolk, though odd examples are found as far off as Winchester, such as Robert Thurberne (1450) at the College. There were smaller workshops in south Suffolk, probably at Ipswich, which produced distinctive but similar brasses to Norwich.

An independent group of engravers worked in the Midlands, from a centre in, or near, Coventry. The school became active between 1480 and 1550. Most of the Midland brasses are peculiar and graceless, though richly decorated and often large. Thomas Andrewe (c.1490) at Charwelton, Northants. (Fig. 93), and Francis Cokayne (1538) at Ashbourne, Derbyshire, are very elaborate, displaying the heavy canopies and comic faces typical of this school. An alabaster tomb with brasses for Henry Foljambe at Chesterfield, Derby, was ordered in 1510 from Henry Harpur and William Moorecock of Burton. There is no proof that the craftsmen did not subcontract for the metal work, and the brasses now on the tomb are restorations of 1879. No conclusions concerning the Midland engravers can be drawn from this evidence.

Another school seems to have had its centre at Bedford or Cambridge. Many of the brasses of Bedfordshire, Cambridgeshire, north Essex and west Suffolk, between the years 1500 to 1530, are engraved in a very simple style. Their execution is cruder than London work of the period, but their design is more pleasing. John Fysher and wife (1528) at Clifton, Beds. (Fig. 91), is a good example, though the ladies are more usually represented wearing flat caps. The placing of the figures beyond the edges of the inscription is a feature of this and other East Anglian schools. A small and peculiar school was apparent-

Fig. 91. John Fysher and wife, 1528. ton, Beds. Length of male effigy 29".

in michaeli futher militis
i A° dm m° cccc rrviii.

ly established in Canterbury during the sixteenth century. Many brasses were engraved by craftsmen unconnected with any large centre. The inscription to the Earl of Murray at St Giles, Edinburgh, was made locally by James Gray, a goldsmith. A collection of seventeenth-century part effigy brasses at Llanrwst, Denbigh, Wales, are signed by William Vaughan and Silvanus Crue. Several Cornish brasses are miserably engraved, while William Attwode (1529) at Doynton, Glos., is clearly the work of an incompetent.

Many continental brasses cannot be associated with particular schools. Of such are the Czarnkowski ancestors (1602) at Czarnkow, Poland, by Valentine Kunink of Posnan, a fine little collection of late fourteenth-century plates at Nordhausen, Germany, and Duncan Liddel (1613) at St Nicholas, Aberdeen, the work of Gaspard Bruydegoms of Antwerp. The destruction of the majority of brasses has only left discernible the pattern of the main centres.

5. *Trade in Brasses*

The outstanding quality of Flemish and Nuremberg brasses created an extraordinary demand for them. Flemish brasses are found in Spain, Portugal and Italy, as well as throughout northern Europe. Nausis, Finland, is the established north-eastern extremity of their distribution. Most are found in churches on the coast or near to large rivers such as the Rhine, Thames or Vistula. The trading fleets of the Hanseatic League of the Baltic Ports must have facilitated the distribution of these monuments. In England particularly large numbers were brought to the Humber and the Wash, and indents abound in the churches of Barton on the Humber, Boston and the marshland churches of Lincolnshire. King's Lynn retains two of its series.

Politics had an influence in this trade. Scottish indents, such as those of Dundrennan and Perth, and the transactions of the Halyburton Ledger, show clearly that Scotland imported Flemish work almost exclusively, so bad were relations with her English neighbours.

Two imported examples in England appear to have been trimmed to local taste. The background of the Kesteven brass (c.1360) at North Mymms, Herts., seems to have been cut away after engraving, while the inscription to the Knevynton brass (1370) at Aveley, Essex, is most probably an English addition.

The Vischer brasses and casts were widely sought after in Poland, the demand being particularly great in Krakow.

One English brass, that of Bishop Hallum of Salisbury, lies at Constance, Germany. Its situation is a product of extraordinary circumstances, as this bishop died attending the famous Council of Constance in 1414. The existence of other English-made brasses at St Patrick's Cathedral, Dublin, Eire, and Bordeaux, France, is explained by the political connections of the time.

Many authorities have held that several of the earliest brasses in England are of French origin, in particular those of Chartham, Horsmonden and Minster-in-Sheppey, Kent, of Trotton, Sussex, and Elsing, Norfolk. The author is not of this view. There was much French influence in English monumental design at the time, sufficient to explain the peculiarities of most of these brasses. The cross-legged pose and unfinished state of the Chartham figure strongly indicate an English origin. The details of the Elsing brass (Fig. 107), especially the subsidiary figures, are so similar to those of the court school stained glass in the north ambulatory of Ely Cathedral (now being moved to St Dunstan's chapel) that a common source in London is most probable. Furthermore the Elsing brass is clearly by the same hand as the Wautone brass (1347) at Wimbish, Essex, in which the figures are represented within an actofoil cross, a peculiarly English form of composition. John de Northwood and a lady at Minster (Fig. 18) are exceptions. The arrangement and detail of the figures and costume, and the position of the knight's shield on the thigh, have no counterpart in English work. It is most probably an import and quite possibly French. A reused fragment on the reverse of Robert Fowler (1540) at St Mary, Islington, London, which shows an angel swinging a censer, is almost certainly French. It is possible that French brasses were brought into England, but in the absence of brasses in France, the supposition cannot be proved.

6. *The Distribution of Brasses*

It is often asked why brasses are so numerous in England in comparison to other countries, and why within England, the concentration in the Home and Eastern Counties is so marked.

In fact there are about 4,000 figure brasses in England and some 400 recorded examples on the Continent. It is certain that more brasses were laid in England than in any other country, though a count of indents would probably modify England's superiority, especially in relation to Flanders. The craft of brass engraving found stronger competition on the Continent than in England. Although the incised slab was a popular monumental

Fig. 92. Joan, Lady Cromwell, c. Tattershall, Lincs. Total length 96".

93. Thomas Andrewe and wife, c.
0. Charwelton, Northants. Total length
"

form, especially in the Midlands, the stone engravers did not master the skill of their fellows in Flanders or France. England has no counterpart to the fantastic collections of slabs at the Abbey of St Bavon at Ghent and the cathedral of Chalons sur Marne in France. Bronze relief casts in Germany far outnumber brasses - there are fifty in Bamberg Cathedral alone - but if these were counted as brasses the numerical comparison would favour Germany. English superiority in this craft is primarily based on number, and this number consists of a high proportion of small figures. It is important to regard continental brasses as examples of small but choice series, the remnants of a manufacture as interesting but less prolific than that of England.

The answer to the second question partly lies in the importation of plate brass. The importation of latton favoured the workshops on the eastern side, the most important being London, York and Norwich. This factor, while not affecting the wealthy, would certainly have influenced the small merchant or landowner in his search for a memorial. There is no marked shortage of sumptuous brasses in the west, Hereford has as many as Buckinghamshire. It is the absence of the modest brass that is so striking. The existing distribution of brasses is somewhat misleading. A full analysis of indents would reveal Lincolnshire and Yorkshire as having been rich in brasses. The preponderance in the Eastern Counties extended further north than now appears.

One supremely important fact is clear from the description of this chapter. The engravers of monumental brasses were not specialists. Brass engraving was the regular or occasional work of monumental sculptors, bell founders and goldsmiths. Whether in England, Flanders, Germany or Poland, the engravers who have been identified are better known for work of a different kind. They were often craftsmen of the highest repute, working in conjunction with famous artists. On account of this fact the identification of engravers and the classification of their work is the most rewarding research open to the student of brasses. Such research can be attempted through a comprehensive collection of rubbings of a period, arranged according to style and scripts, which can be compared with other art forms and related to available documentary evidence.

4 THE DESIGN OF BRASSES

An understanding of the engraver's work is an essential preliminary to an appreciation of the design and arrangement of brasses. As has been described, the brass engravers were themselves casters or sculptors, or worked in collaboration with stone masons, and their products reflect this close association of skills. Brasses were generally designed to represent in line the forms and details of sculpture or relief.

Fig. 94. Detail of Fig. 88 showing a feas of wild men.

All the main features of the latton cast tombs of English royalty in the Confessor Chapel at Westminster Abbey can be found reproduced on elaborate medieval figure brasses. These features consist of the recumbent effigy, the head canopy with shafts filled with subsidiary figures, the patterned background and the inscription forming a border. Figures of mourning relatives - weepers - and shields of arms decorate the sides of the tombs. The engravers sought to reproduce such arrangements in their finest work, and achieved the required effect through various conventions. The lofty vertical canopies of many sculptured tombs were treated as being horizontal, and as a consequence canopies on brasses are usually more elaborate than the horizontal head canopies of sculpture. The decorations of tomb chests - the weepers and shields – were incorporated within and around the canopies. Various devices were used to simulate the appearance of depth. The limbs of many Flemish figures protrude over the shafts and bases of the canopies. The sword of Duke Premislaus crosses the canopy shaft, while that of King Eric is represented as being under the canopy. The inner vaults of the canopies are often represented. Crude perspective is attempted in many canopies, as for example on that of Alan Fleming at Newark (c.1361). Occasionally the base of the figure was placed below the base of the canopy shafts, as on the brass of Abbot Estney at Westminster Abbey. Renaissance and later brasses had a similar though remoter connection with contemporary sculptures. Cross-hatching to simulate shadow and give an impression of solidity was being used on brasses extensively after 1500.. The relationship between sculptured tomb and brass design can be traced throughout their history. The following are a few significant examples. The brass of Duke Premislaus at Lubiaz was clearly inspired by the tomb of Duke Henry IV of Silesia at Wroclaw. The elaborate canopy of Sir Hugh Hastings at Elsing (Fig. 107), with its rich pediment and brackets, has its stone counterpart

ig. 95. Detail of Fig. 88 showing a wild-
an carrying off a lady.

in the horizontal canopies of Aymer de Valence (1326) at Westminster Abbey and Eleanor Percy (c.1345) at Beverley, Yorks. The flattened representation of the hands, one being folded across the other, which was generally used on Flemish brasses during the latter half of the fourteenth century, appears in sculpture at the Jerusalem Church at Bruges. The designs of German relief casts are reproduced precisely on brasses. The English Tudor wall brass, showing the deceased kneeling at a prayer desk, has many sculptured equivalents such as the tomb of John Dawtry (1527) at Petworth, Sussex. Brass engravers did not only imitate sculpture. Their works often filled a special place in sculptured compositions. Tudor canopied recessed tombs were more usually enriched with brass than with carved effigies.

This comparison must not be pressed too far. The pictorial possibilities of the engraved medium were appreciated, and particularly in Flemish work the limitations of sculpture were not allowed to cramp the decorative ideas of the engravers. Several sixteenth-century brasses were designed on paintings. In England during the late sixteenth and the seventeenth centuries a type of brass was made with close affinities to the copper plate engravings of the book illustrators, which had little connection with monumental art. Nevertheless the general assessment is fair, and the engraver's intentions can usually be clarified by reference to sculptured or relief memorials.

Changes in thought and ideals which influenced fine art and architecture are reflected in the design of brasses. From 1250 to 1480 brasses were essentially Gothic and monumental in their form. The deceased were represented in a conventional idealized manner. Until c.1410 the main engraving lines tended to be bold, deep and severe. Canopies were lofty in their arrangement even when composed of massed tabernacles. From c.1410 to c.1450 brasses achieved great gracefulness, though the engraving lines became finer and less confident. From 1450 to 1480 the influence of late Gothic became oppressively evident in a coarsening of line and heaviness, and confusion in architectural detail. Realist influence after 1470 effected changes in continental brasses. Both in Flanders and Germany the deceased were often represented as alive in a domestic or workday setting (Fig. 69), their features being natural rather than conventional. The brasses of Hermann Vischer are outstanding in this respect. The desire for realism produced the morbid concentration on death reflected in cadavers and shroud

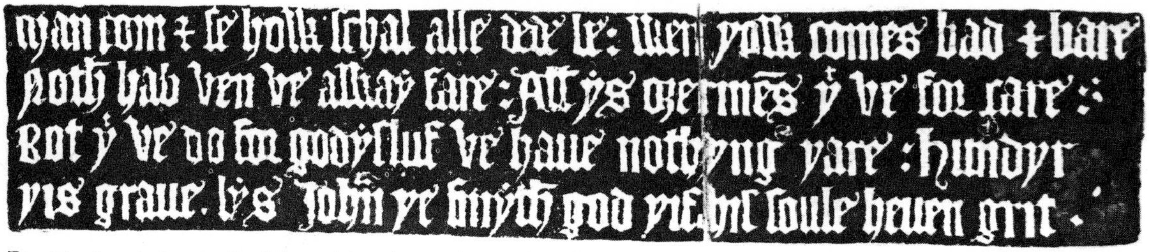

Fig. 96. Inscription in English to John the smith, c. 1370. Brightwell Baldwin, Oxon. Size 21″ x 4″.

figures. Renaissance influence was reflected in brasses only gradually. Classical detail of both architectural and decorative forms appears on brasses about 1520 but was not generally adopted until the middle of the century. English brasses are particularly conservative in this respect. The Italian sculptors invited to England by Henry VII had little general influence, and Renaissance art filtered into England through Flemish and German contact. The canopies of William Porter (1524) and Edmund Frowsetoure (1529) at Hereford Cathedral exhibit the first indication of Renaissance ideas. While in their detail and architecture, brasses of the late sixteenth century were classical, their overall design tended to remain traditional.

The major workshops arranged the composition of brasses with a consistent but different emphasis. In London work, the figure and the base inscription were the objects of concentration. The canopy was normally light and of secondary importance. In Flemish work, the canopy and background were far more substantial and intricate, and when the traceried canopies of the fourteenth century lost their popularity, their place was taken by heraldry and other features which tended to overwhelm the figures. In both Saxony and northern Germany, though not in the Rhineland, the canopy was treated as a framework only, and the compositions were dominated by large figures and surrounded by elaborate borders. French work seems to have had affinities with Flanders in its overall composition, but the detail was restrained by simpler backgrounds. While the quality of Flemish engraving remained excellent, the intricacy of Flemish composition was not well suited to the overlay of cross-hatching and fussy detail of the sixteenth century. In contrast German composition could bear this detail. Flemish design is seen at its best in brasses of the fourteenth century, but German design in those of the sixteenth century. English design is seen at its finest in the fourteenth and early fifteenth century. Its subsequent

Fig. 97. Merchant's mark of Walter man, 1521. Kempsford, Glos. Detail.

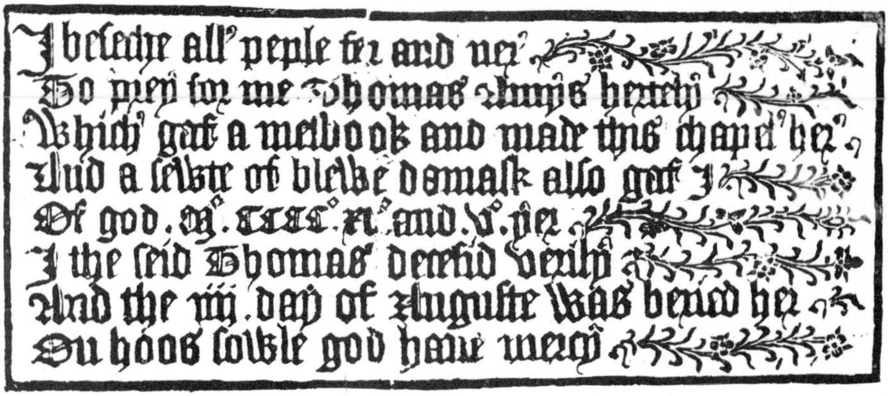

Fig. 98. Inscription in English to Thomas Amys, c. 1495. Barton Turf, Norfolk. Size 18½" x 8".

decline resulted from a general deterioration of technique and stagnation of ideas within the craft.

The Inscription

An inscription stating the particulars of the deceased is the most essential part of any monument. Many brasses consist simply of an inscription recording the name and date of death and concluding with a short prayer. Such small plates abound in Norfolk and Suffolk churches. An inscription at Ashbourne, Derby., concerning the dedication of the church in 1241, is probably the earliest surviving English engraved brass, while inscription plates continued to be laid throughout the eighteenth and nineteenth centuries. The earliest recorded brass is an inscription of 1189 on an altar at St Ememeram, Regensburg. Inscriptions took two main forms, being rectangular or extending into a border strip. These borders were often set at an angle - in chamfer - around the edges of tombs. The lettering was either incised or engraved into relief. The language of the majority of inscriptions during the fourteenth century was Latin, though Norman French was generally used in England until 1340 and remained in use to the early fifteenth century. Much French was apparently used on French brasses, and Flemish brasses exhibit a wide range of languages including Spanish. The first inscription in English (c.1370) appears at Brightwell Baldwin, Oxon. (Fig. 96). Latin was generally used during the first half of the fifteenth century, though the vernacular gained popularity by 1500. Interest in Latin revived during the sixteenth century.

The type of script used varied according to period. Rounded Lombardic capitals were used exclusively until 1330. These were often separately inlaid around the border and remain largely intact at Lubiaz (Fig. 13). Many English indents record such inscriptions exactly, and that of Lady Joan de Cobham has been completely restored. Gothic 'black letter' script superceded Lombardic about 1340 and remained in use into the sixteenth century. This script varied in form, appearing bold and rounded in the fourteenth century, stiff in the fifteenth and heavy and elaborate in the sixteenth century. Much fifteenth century Flemish lettering is exquisite in its execution. Arabic numerals were used frequently between 1440 and 1500. Roman script was introduced through Renaissance influence during the first half of the sixteenth century and gradually replaced black letter.

Fig. 99. Man in armour, c. 1300. Crof Lincs. Length 18″.

The content of inscriptions is a particularly interesting study. Most early examples are simple, identifying the deceased, recording a pious invocation for the dead and occasionally offering a pardon in return for the saying of prayers. Inscriptions became more complex in the late fourteenth and fifteenth centuries. Many are written in elegiac or rhyming Leonine verse. Some record the achievements of the deceased. The example of Thomas Amys (1495) at Barton Turf, Norfolk (Fig. 98), is particularly attractive, recording that he 'gaf a mesbook and made this chapel her and a sewte of blewe damask also gaf . . .' The Reformation brought an end in England to the pious intention of inscriptions, which often became lengthy flatteries of the commemorated. Much curious information is included. Of young John Byrd (1629) at Headcorn, Kent, is written '. . . and in the time of his sicknesse deliverd many godly exortations to his parents takinge his leave of them with such unexpected ex-pres-sions as are not common in so younge a child.' The contractions and abbreviations used make the reading of many inscriptions difficult, and many of these are dealt with in detail in J. Franklyn's book *Brasses*.

Although functional in purpose, inscriptions were also treated most decoratively. Many English border inscriptions are enriched with animals, birds, insects and emblems. Inscriptions at Northleach (1447) and Tormarton (1493), Glos., are particularly rich in creatures. Heraldic devices also occur as stops between the words, such as the elephant of Viscount Beaumont (1507) at Wivenhoe, Essex. Occasionally initial letters are decorated, at Berkhampstead, Herts. (c.1500), with a figure of St Jerome, or at Worstead, Norfolk (1440), with a humorous face. Flemish inscriptions, both border and rectangular types, are often superbly decorated. The great border inscription to Peter Lansame (1489) at the Hospice Notre Dame at Ypres, Belgium, is unsurpassed, the words weaving around representations of the ages of man.

Fig. 100. Civilian, c. 1370. Deddingto Oxford. Length 18″.

Fig. 101. Joan Plessi, c. 1360. Quainton, Bucks. Length 9".

The inscription at Leça do Balio, Portugal, is surrounded with grotesques, medallions, saints and a representation of the Annunciation.

The Figure

The deceased when represented was usually shown full figure. A large number of English brasses, especially those to parish priests, were made in half or three-quarter effigy. A selection of four fourteenth-century half-effigies is illustrated, including a very early knight from Croft, Lincs. (Figs 99-102). The earliest surviving bust is at Blickling, Norfolk (c.1360), to a civilian. While many of these part figures were made for economy, there was clearly a fashion for such representation. Several are very large, as Roger Campedene (1398) at Stanford in the Vale, Berks. Such representation lasted until the seventeenth century, those of the York school in the late sixteenth century being particularly elaborate.

Until the close of the fifteenth century most figures were represented as recumbent. Their heads often rest on cushions or helmets, while their feet rest on the various devices described in Chapter 2. The resting pose is emphasized by the placing of the feet. On some brasses, at Shernbourne, Norfolk (1458), for instance, the heels are shown completely clear of the rest, emphasising the recumbent posture. It is often alleged that a plot of earth with grass and flowers at the feet indicated a standing position. This view is unsupportable. Most English civilians from the fourteenth to the sixteenth centuries are shown resting against such ground, which was as conventional a rest as the lion or hound. Representation of the feet unsupported was used on the Continent, for example at Lubiaz and Ghent, but was not popular in England.

The hands are usually shown in prayer, placed together, held upwards and apart or, as in the Flemish convention, folded one over the other. Occasionally the hands grasp a sword, sceptre, chalice or other symbol of office. Repose is sometimes indicated by a downward folding of the hands, as at Wensley, Yorks. (c.1360), and Fulbourne, Cambs. (1477). The holding of hands between husband and wife is a particularly pleasing English arrangement, with examples at Southacre, Norfolk (1384) (Fig. 24), Little Shelford, Cambs. (c.1410), and Trotton, Sussex (1419). German brasses often show the arms upraised holding croziers or representations of buildings (Fig. 103).

During the early fourteenth century a general appearance of vitality was given to the figure, the agile cross-legged posture of English brasses from 1280 to 1320 and

Fig. 102. A priest, c. 1340. Great Brington, Northants. Length 19".

the sway at the hips from 1320 to 1350 being particularly effective. After 1450 kneeling figures became quite common, but these generally form part of a devotional composition in which the deceased is represented kneeling before the Blessed Virgin or a patron saint. An early example, actually forming a latton altar piece, is at Susa, Italy. John Stathum and wife (1454) at Morley, Derby., kneeling below a figure of St Christopher, is a typical English example.

Changing ideas at the close of the fifteenth century influenced figure representation. Thomas Pownder (1525) at Ipswich (Fig. 45) and Andrew Evyngar (1533) at All Hallows, Barkyng, are excellent Flemish brasses showing two families in reverent prayer, the main figures standing in natural poses. The earlier Schelewaerts brass at Bruges representing the doctor actually at work is a vital composition (Fig. 69). It is in the treatment of the detail of the figure, however, rather than in the setting, that the change is most marked. In Nuremberg work in particular, the figures are brought to life by the sensitive treatment of the hands, the expression on the faces and the pose. The half-profile view and asymmetrical placing of the feet adds to the vital impression. Movement in the drapery was indicated by its accurate representation. The vertical fall of the dress, laboured in fifteenth-century brasses, was superceded by realistic arrangement. The influence of Dürer's art in these matters was profound. In contrast, much Flemish and most English work remained static. English early Tudor brasses have an extremely stiff appearance. This suits the heraldic wall brasses, showing figures kneeling in tabards and mantles at prayer desks, which form the most attractive English work of the period. An occasional figure is well represented, as Sir Thomas Bullen (1538) at Hever, Kent (Fig. 33), and the Fermour group of brasses. Nevertheless English brasses overall reveal the features of a conservative and deteriorating craft.

From the middle of the sixteenth century to the seventeenth century two different aims were followed by the engravers. The majority of English figures, for all the shading, the attempted portraiture and other realistic detail engraved upon them, appear as lifeless as their predecessors. The finest Caroline brasses at Chigwell, Essex, Penn, Bucks., Stopham, Sussex (Fig. 34), and East Sutton, Kent, are remarkably traditional in their arrangement. Only the children's figures have any vitality. In surprising contrast are the considerable number of brasses representing the deceased in unusual attitu-

Fig. 103. Bishop Yso von Wilpe, 1231. St Andrews, Verden, Germany. Length 78″ German work.

04. Shield and inscription to William e, 1389. All Hallows, Barkyng, Lon- Diameter 11".

105. Howling beasts, from the back- d of Bishops Burchard von Serken John von Mul, 1350. Lübeck Cathedral, any. Detail. Flemish work.

des. John Pendarves (1617) at St Michael, Oxford, rises to dispute for his degree, Alexander Strange (1620) at Buntingford, Herts., preaches to his congregation, and Thomas Montagu (1630) at Winkfield, Berks., hands bread to the poor. Many kneeling figures, their families arranged behind them, are beautifully and sensitively engraved. This contrast appears on continental work. Pierre de Valencia (1615) at St Jacques, Bruges, is in the monumental tradition, his head resting on a cushion. Duncan Liddel (1613) at Aberdeen is shown seated at his desk, surrounded by his instruments and books.

It would seem that the recumbent figure brass was well suited to the conventional and idealistic treatment of the medieval engraver. It was not so well suited to the naturalistic treatment increasingly demanded after 1520. Had the engravers abandoned the old tradition, their intentions would have found clearer expression. This tradition was apparently too well established and taste too conservative to make this possible. As a result the most imaginative late brasses are often of the poorest quality. The tradition has remained. The brasses of the nineteenth-century Gothic revival are throwbacks to fourteenth-century ideas.

Heraldry and Merchant Marks

Many brasses are decorated with shields. These vary in shape according to period, early shields being pointed, sixteenth-century and later examples having a shallower curve. Tilting shields with a recess for the lance are occasionally represented, as at Stoke Poges, Bucks (1476). Sixteenth and seventeenth-century heraldic devices are often displayed on lozenges or within an oval.

Shields are of three main kinds, namely the family arms, Merchant Company and City arms, or private trading or merchant marks. Family arms are by far the most numerous and occur on most substantial military or civil brasses. The others are principally found on the brasses of English merchants, especially during the fifteenth and sixteenth centuries. The arms of the Merchant Adventurers, incorporated in 1296, and the arms of Ipswich appear above Thomas Pownder at Ipswich (Fig. 45). His personal trading mark is placed in the centre. Arms of the Mercers Company, incorporated in 1394, appear above John Lambard at Hinxworth, and his private mark below (Fig. 42). Among other company arms represented are those of the Goldsmiths, the Skinners, the Grocers, the Drapers, the Haberdashers, the Merchant Tailors, the Salters and the Brewers. Many of the brasses with such shields are found near London, Nor--

wich and Bristol, or in connection with the brasses of woolmen. Merchant marks on brasses usually consist of a device into which are worked the initials of the owner. They have been admirably described and illustrated by F. A. Girling in *English Merchants' Marks*, O.U.P., 1964. Heraldic shields were engraved with great accuracy, and are often sufficiently precise to identify the deceased. The heraldic colours, azure (blue), gules (red), sable (black), vert (green) and purpure (purple), were originally inlaid in coloured resins or enamels. The metals, or (gold) and argent (silver), were represented respectively by the brass surface and lead inlay. Fur was usually represented by engraved lead inlay. The reader is referred to a manual of heraldry for a description of heraldic charges and their usage.

Shields were usually placed above and below the figures, or above and below the canopy. On some particularly fine brasses, for example at Westminster Abbey (1399), Little Horkesley, Essex (1412), and Enfield, Middx. (c.1470), the shields are represented as secured to the canopy shafts. On many Flemish examples the shields are supported by angels above the heads of the deceased, while on German brasses the shield is usually placed at the feet, often in a slanting position. Crested helms and manteling were often placed above the shields on elaborate brasses, the Nowemiasto brass being a superb example of this feature.

Many brasses consist of no more than an inscription and a shield of arms. The shield of William Tonge (1389), surrounded by a circular inscription, at All Hallows, Barkyng, is a simple but striking memorial (Fig. 104). The inscription with shield, helm and manteling, is another common combination. Many extremely large continental compositions are arranged around a heraldic centre. There are four such brasses at St Elizabeth, Marburg, Germany. Several Flemish shields are finely displayed by angels, as at St Jacques, Bruges, and Nieuport.

Banners were occasionally represented as a heraldic feature above the canopies. English examples are found at Ashford, Kent (1375), Lingfield, Surrey (1420, restored), and West Grinstead, Sussex (1441).

The use of heraldic devices on costume and as foot rests has been described in Chapter 2. The use of shields purely decoratively as a background is described later in this chapter. It is interesting to note that the English brass engravers' finest surviving heraldic work was not for a monumental purpose, but for the stall plates of the Knights of the Garter at St George's Chapel, Windsor.

Fig. 106. Head of a bishop or abbot, c 1375. The British Museum, London. Length 28''. Flemish work. Rubbing by H. F. Owen Evans.

The Canopy

Many brasses are elaborated with one or more canopies surrounding the figures. These canopies consist of an arch, the soffit, above which usually rises an ogival arch. The curve of the soffit is diversified by protruding cusps, while the ogive outer arch is decorated with projecting leaf ornaments, crockets, meeting at the apex in a finial. The space between the two arches is filled with tracery. The complete gable is described as the pediment. Canopies exist with as many as six pediments. The pediment is flanked by shafts which are extended into pinnacles. Occasionally the shafts support an upper or super canopy. Although these canopies form part of a horizontal design, they were often modelled on vertical stone canopies, and minor inconsistencies may be noted, such as the hanging shields on the canopy of the Duchess of Gloucester at Westminster Abbey.

The most elaborate canopies, especially those of the fourteenth-century Bruges school, support a series of tabernacles above the pediments. These tabernacles are filled with representations of the Deity, attendant angels and other figures (Fig. 106). English examples are generally simpler, the tabernacles enclosing a representation of the Blessed Virgin and Christ child, or the Holy Trinity with attendant saints. The brasses at Cobham (1407) (Fig. 21) and Cowfold (1433) (Fig. 68) are beautiful examples. Representations occasionally occupy the centre of the pediment, as at Elsing (1347) (Fig. 107), or take the place of the finial, as at Cobham (1395). Super canopies sometimes take the form of a row of tabernacles, for example at Boston, Lincs. (1398), but a parapet of battlements is more common. On many of the finest brasses, the canopy shafts are widened to enclose niches filled with saints, prophets or weepers. Saints and prophets are depicted at Schwerin, and weepers at Elsing (Fig. 107). Among the Elsing figures is King Edward III wearing his crown and a jupon with the quartered arms of France and England. Members of the bishop's household including a huntsman and a miner with his pick and bag, fill the shafts around Bishop Novak (1456) at Wroclaw.

The earliest canopies were usually of straight gable form, as at Cobham (1320) (Fig. 108) and on the Trotton indent (Fig. 36). The ogive arch superceded this form in the early fourteenth century and remained in use until the sixteenth century, though late Gothic canopies are very cumbersome with large crockets and deep vaulting. Classical architectural forms replaced Gothic in the mid-sixteenth century, but appear principally on continental brasses.

There are many unusual forms of canopy, among which a semi-circular canopy at Ashford (1375) and a canopy drawn on the design of a ship's quarter at Stoke Fleming, Devon (1391), are particularly interesting. Interlaced tree branches form the canopy on many of the brasses made in Nuremberg. A castle forms the canopy of Bishop Wyvil at Salisbury (Fig. 11).

Pictorial Panels

A peculiar but most interesting feature of many Flemish canopied brasses of the fourteenth century are decorative panels beneath the figures. These panels form a base to the canopy and represent worldly, mythical or religious subjects.

Hunting scenes appear below Alan Fleming at Newark. Country pastimes and labour are represented on Adam de Walsokne's brass at King's Lynn. The brass of Robert Braunche, also at King's Lynn, has a long panel depicting a peacock feast with musicians entertaining the diners. At Schwerin, Germany, and Torun, Poland, are shown the feasts and maraudings of forest wild men (wodehouses). The Schwerin example is particularly detailed, depicting the abduction of a lady by a wodehouse who is hotly pursued by a mounted knight (Fig. 95).

Religious panels showing scenes from the lives of St Nicholas and St Eloy, the latter depicted pinching the Devil's nose, are engraved below the feet of Bishops Serken and Mul at Lübeck Cathedral. The purpose of including such scenes seems to have been decorative.

Background

The engraved background is an important feature of most rectangular sheet brasses. The detail of Flemish plates is especially rich. The two most common Flemish motifs of the fourteenth century were geometric patterns enlivened with birds and small animals or rows of howling monsters (Fig. 105). Fifteenth-century backgrounds generally consisted of elaborate floral or leaf decoration or a pattern of emblems and mottos. The background to most German examples was formed by a curtain embroidered with pomegranates.

The bare stone usually forms the background to separate inlay compositions. There are, however, several English examples where a profusion of shields of arms, heraldic devices or small scrolls provide a decorative setting (Fig. 109). The indent of Margaret de Camoys at Trotton is powdered with shields and stars. The brass of Richard

Fig. 107. Sir Hugh Hastings, 1347. sing, Norfolk. Total length 102″. Deta angel by the head at present in the aut. possession.

108. Lady Joan de Cobham, c. 1320.
...am, Kent. Length 97″.

Wylloughby (1471) at Wollaton, Notts., has a background of whelk shells. Thirty-one scrolls bearing the words 'Jesus' and 'Mercy' surround the figure of Sir John de Brewys (1426) at Wiston, Sussex.

Representations in perspective of room interiors, colonnades' and other architectural features are common backgrounds for sixteenth and seventeenth-century brasses. English rectangular plates are remarkable in their simplicity. Many have plain backgrounds, a feature rarely met on the Continent.

The Border

A decorative border is a feature of rectangular sheet brasses. Usually the ornament consists of no more than a series of flowers and stops or a pattern of foliage. Occasionally the decoration is more extensive. A Jesse tree forms the border at Schwerin (1375) and St Catherine, Lübeck (1474) (Fig. 110). Martin van der Capelle at Bruges Cathedral has a border engraved with horses' bits. All three are of Flemish work. Mrs Dorothy Williams (1694) at Pimperne, Dorset, is an unusual English example, having a border decorated with symbols of mortality.

The border acquired greatest importance in the designs used by the Hilligers at Freiberg and Dresden. The later brasses at Meissen and all the Freiberg series have magnificent borders, filled with shields, arabesques, amorini, birds and sea monsters.

Devotional Panels

Representations of saints, angels and the Deity have been described in their relation to canopy design. Religious representations have an important place as the focal point of many compositions. The brass may show the commemorated kneeling in prayer and presented by a patron saint to the person adored. Robert Honywode (1522) at Windsor is an excellent example (Fig. 113). The canon kneels at a faldstool aided by St Catherine. His prayer, 'virgo tuū natū p me p'cor ora beatū', pleading for intercession, is addressed on a scroll to the crowned figure of Mary, who holds the Christ child and a sceptre. George Rede at Fovant, Wilts., directs his prayer to a representation of the Annunciation (Fig. 112). Such devotional memorials are common in the early sixteenth century. There are good examples at Dendermonde, Belgium, Aachen Cathedral, Germany and St Patrick's Cathedral, Dublin. In two examples the figure of the supplicant is dwarfed, by a large figure of Christ holding an orb at Emden and by the figure of St Henry of Finland at Nausis.

On most English brasses the devotional panels are on

Fig. 109. Henry Grene and wife, 1467. Lo-wick, Northants. Total length 90″. Illustration from Monumental Brass Society portfolio.

Fig. 110. John Lüneborch, 1474. St Catherine, Lübeck, Germany. Length 112″. Flemish work. Illustration from Creeny.

Fig. 111. The visit of the Sheph c.1500. Cobham, Surrey. Size 4½″ x Rubbing by H. F. Owen Evans.

Fig. 112. George Rede kneeling before a representation of the Annunciation, c. 1500. Fovant, Wilts. Size 14¾" x 12¼". Rubbing by H. F. Owen Evans.

Fig. 113. Canon Robert Honywode, 1522. St George's Chapel, Windsor, Berks. Length 24". Rubbing by H. F. Owen Evans.

Fig. 114. The Resurrection, from a brass to Robert Harding, 1503. Cranley, Surrey. Detail, 8" x 8".

Fig. 115. Chalice brass to Henry Alik 1502. Colney, Norfolk. Length of cha 4½".

small plates introduced above the figures, which are arranged in a recumbent or kneeling position. Scrolls inscribed with prayers issue from heads or hands. The panels are often curiously engraved and cover a wide range of subjects.

Fig. 116. Robert de Paris and wife kneel before a cross with the Holy Trinity head, 1408. Hildersham, Cambs. T length 66".

Representations of the Holy Trinity are most common. These depict God the Father as a bearded man holding the crucified Christ between his knees (Fig. 21). The Holy Spirit is usually shown as a dove perched on an arm of the cross. There are three such plates at Childrey, Berks., and a particularly fine one at Stoke Charity, Hants. (1483). The Holy Trinity in a verbal representation occurs on shields at Cowfold, Sussex (Fig. 68), and St Cross, Winchester. Scenes from the life of the Blessed Virgin are numerous; for example, Mary with Christ at Brampton, Norfolk (1468), the Annunciation at March, Cambs. (1507), and the Pieta at Carshalton, Surrey (1497). Scenes from the life of Christ are uncommon but varied, for example, the visitation of the Shepherds to the stable at Cobham, Surrey (c.1500) (Fig. 111), the Crucifixion at Chelsfield, Kent (1417, mutilated), the Resurrection, at Swansea, Glamorgan (c.1500), and Cranley, Surrey (1503) (Fig. 114), and Christ seated in glory on a rainbow at Sibson, Leicester (1532). Christ standing in blessing is represented at Mereworth, Kent (1542).

Figures of saints are occasionally found; St Christopher several times at Morley, Derbyshire, St John at Beaumaris, Anglesey, and most interesting, St Ethelbert, king and martyr, at Hereford Cathedral. St Ethelbert is shown seated holding his crowned head in his left hand. It is a very early brass (c.1290), the only remaining fragment of the brass to Bishop Thomas de Cantilupe. The mass of St. Gregory is illustrated at Macclesfield, Cheshire (1506).

Devotional panels and compositions suffered particularly severely during the sixteenth-century iconoclasm.

Emblem Brasses

There are two large groups of brasses which commemorate the deceased by an inscription and emblem. These are the heart and chalice brasses.

Heart brasses were apparently laid to record the burial of the heart only, the corpse having been buried elsewhere. This circumstance arose from chance or the expressed wish of the deceased. Hearts are sometimes represented simply, as at Trunch, Norfolk (c.1530), but more often shown held by hands. Inscribed scrolls are often placed as issuing from the heart.

Chalice brasses were laid in memory of priests, depicting the chalice alone or with the eucharistic wafer. The earliest English examples are in Yorkshire, but the majority are found in Norfolk (Fig. 115). Many of the Norfolk chalices are engraved on rectangular plates. Hands are occasionally shown grasping the base of the chalice.

The emblem of the rose was used, though only one example now exists. This is at Edlesborough, Bucks., and is probably wrongfully associated with an inscription of 1412.

Emblems of trade or profession are occasionally found, such as the gloves of Peter Denot (1440), a glover, at Fletching, Sussex, and the warship of Roger Morris (1615) at Margate, Kent. Morris was one of the six principal masters of attendance of His Majesty's navy royal. The emblem of the naked soul borne heavenwards in a sheet by angels is the memorial of Walter Beauchamp (c.1430) at Checkendon, Oxon.

Symbols of the Evangelists

The symbols of the four Evangelists, the winged figures of the lion of St Mark, the bull of St Luke, the eagle of St John and the angel of St Matthew were normally placed at the four corners of marginal inscriptions. They were set in quatrefoils, circles or, more rarely, in shields.

These symbols were also laid around brasses with foot inscriptions and are handsomely displayed round the half-effigy of Roger Campedene at Stanford in the Vale, Berks.

Crosses and Brackets

Two important types of brass, the cross and bracket brasses, have a common feature in a supporting shaft or column. They are, however, entirely different in both origin and conception.

Crosses, engraved or carved on tomb slabs, were widely used in the twelfth century. This simple and symbolic decoration was the model for the cross brasses.

Several crosses of straight Latin form remain, the cross arms terminating with fleur de lys. A long and graceful example commemorates Roger Cheyne (1414) at Cassington, Oxon. At Broadwater, Sussex (1445), the arms are inscribed, and at Higham Ferrers, Northants. (1400), the fine cross to Thomas Chichele is decorated with symbols of the Evangelists at the terminals and a representation of the Deity at the intersection. A curious cross at Eversley, Hants. (1502), is engraved as if constructed of chain links. A few crosses in Kent are completely plain. More elaborate are crosses opening out into a head which contains figures. It is very possible that the placing of figures within the cross head developed from the early slab design in which a half-figure or bust was placed above the cross, as found in the slab at Winchester Cathedral to Prior Basynge (1295). The earliest of these crosses - at Merton College, Oxford, and Chinnor, Oxon. (both c.1320) - show part-figures respectively over and within a cross. Fleur de lys decorate the extremities of the arms. Most crosses have quatrefoil or octofoil heads, enclosing small full length figures. The inscribed cross at Woodchurch, Kent (c.1330), is a fine quatrefoil, while the cross at Hildersham, Cambs. (1408), has an elaborate octofoil head. The place of honour at Hildersham is taken by the Holy Trinity, while Robert Parys and wife kneel below (Fig. 116). John Mulsho and wife (1400) at Newton-by-Geddington, Northants., similarly kneel below St Faith, who stands in the cross head. Other crosses with figures are at Taplow, Bucks. (c.1350), St Michael's, St Alban's (c.1400), Stone, Kent (1408), and Buxted, Sussex (1408).

Bracket brasses seem to have derived their form from architectural wall brackets. Just as the sculptured bracket supported a figure of a saint under a canopy, so the brass imitated the design.

Most surviving bracket brasses represent the deceased standing on a cusped bracket raised by a shaft. Canopies are shown on the finest examples, which are at Bray, Berks. (1378) (Fig. 117), Merton College, Oxford (c. 1420), and Cotterstock, Northants. (1420). In contrast, John Strete (1405) at Upper Hardres, Kent, kneels at the base praying to St Peter and St Paul, who stand on the bracket. A similar but much mutilated composition is at Burford, Oxon. The large number of indents of similar style at Burford prove that this arrangement was not unusual. The Norwich engravers made bracket brasses in very curious forms. St John Maddermarket, Norwich, has two notable designs. The Terry family (1524) stand on brackets rising from a tree trunk, and John Marsham and wife (1525) stand on a bracket shaped like a table, its top strewn with bones.

The shafts of cross and bracket brasses are very similar,

Fig. 118. Walter Curson and wife, c. Waterperry, Oxon. The brass is mad reused portions of the brass of S Kamp, 1442. Total length 98".

though the cross shafts are usually longer. The shafts are sometimes ornamented or inscribed and often decorated with pairs of leaves. Steps form the most usual bases to the shafts. A fox, a punning allusion to the name of the deceased, supports the shaft at Bray. The Taplow cross - to a fishmonger - springs from the back of a dolphin. A large, unusual cross at Grainthorpe, Lincs., has a base of rock surrounded with swimming fish.

Cross and bracket brasses are now rare, but this is the effect of deliberate destruction. Their shape made them particularly offensive to the Reformers. All the brasses of these types known to the author are of English workmanship, though Latin crosses were undoubtedly also made by the continental engravers. The indents of Ely, St Alban's and Salisbury Cathedrals reveal the original splendour of these brasses more clearly than the few that remain.

Allegorical Designs

The inclusion of allegorical subjects in brass design became quite popular by the end of the sixteenth century. The English artist Robert Haydock, who is particularly associated with such work, signed the plate of Erasmus Williams (1608) at Tingewick, Bucks., and his initials appear on the brass of Henry Airay (1616) at the Queen's College, Oxford. The remarkable feature of brasses of this kind is the relationship between the inscription and the background. The inscription contains similes and biblical references related to the deceased, which are intricately represented on the background. Provost Airey, likened to Elisha in his inscription, is surrounded by scenes of Elisha's miracles. These brasses are very lightly engraved and share in both texture and design the qualities of contemporary copper plates for book illustration.

Allegory on brasses has a longer history on the theme of the triumph of death. A discourse with death is recorded on the inscription of John Rudyng (1481) at Biggleswade, Beds., and Death's skeleton figure with darts forms part of the much mutilated composition. James Gray (1591), a keeper of the park at Hunsdon, Herts., is represented shooting a stag with a cross bow as Death strikes him in turn with a dart. William Strode (1649) at Shepton Mallet, Somerset, protests as Death rises to strike his wife.

Only the main aspects of monumental brass design have been described, and these have been treated very generally. The study of design is ideal for the collector of rubbings, who can make precise comparisons and observations from illustrations at hand.

5 DESTRUCTION AND RESTORATION

While existing brasses offer limitless interest, it is essential to realize that they are a small fraction of the number originally laid. The total number engraved cannot be assessed accurately, but the evidence of indents and historical records indicate a European total of over two hundred thousand. The destruction of brasses arose from a variety of circumstances.

The fierceness of religious controversy in the sixteenth and seventeenth centuries stimulated the destruction of church ornaments and fittings, which were regarded as idolatrous and superstitious. Secular powers took advantage of the situation to acquire treasure. The ministers of Henry VIII and his son Edward VI were particularly active in this matter. The suppression of the smaller monasteries in 1536 and the Dissolution of the larger monastic houses in 1539 led to the removal of great quantities of brasses. The parish churches suffered particularly in the reign of Edward. Many brasses were melted down and the slabs often used for domestic purposes. Robert, Earl of Sussex, used the brasses and slabs from Attleborough, Norfolk, as paving. Some brasses had particular features obliterated, while others were mutilated by the erasure of pious phrases in the inscription and the removal of religious representations. These were often the efforts of relatives to save the monument from total destruction. The brasses at All Hallows Barkyng, London, have been treated in this fashion. In the Netherlands the Calvinist iconoclasm of 1566 caused widespread havoc. The Scottish Calvinists despoiled the churches. Many churches were sacked during the French religious civil wars. Further depredations followed in the seventeenth century. During the English civil war and the Commonwealth, many cathedral churches, Canterbury, Rochester and Lincoln in particular, were robbed of their brasses. The destruction of 'popish' ornaments was general. William Dowsing, the notorious Parliamentary Visitor in East Anglia, destroyed 192 brasses in Suffolk alone between 1643 and 1644. The prevailing disregard for church monuments is revealed in the brass of Lettice Barnarde (1593) at Newnham Murren, Oxon., which has been struck by musket balls.

Re-used brasses, commonly known as palimpsests, are a salvage from this destruction. Much of the looted plate was sold to brass engravers who used it again in a variety of ways. Instances of brasses having been reversed and re-engraved occur as early as the fourteenth cen-

Figs. 119-120. Inscription to Jane Bra[...] 1539, and reverse fragment of a bishop [...] abbot, c. 1430. Eaton Bray, Beds. S[...] 15″ x 5″.

I·Iane the doughter of edmond lord Bray
vnder this stone lieth closed In clay
alle ye my frendys I pray you pray for me
like as ye ar so I was + as I am so shall ye be
obyt b̄ die marcij an° dni m°cccc° xxxix

tury at Clifton Campville, Staffs., and Topcliffe, Yorks. The practice became common in the fifteenth century.

1. *Wasters*

Wasters are brasses which were rejected for some fault in the engraving, and never left the workshop. Good examples are the coped priest, Thomas Cod (1465) at St Margaret's, Rochester, Kent, and the hunting scene above John Selwyn (1587) at Walton on Thames, Surrey, where an idential subject appears on both sides, clearly engraved by the same craftsman but differing in detail.

2. *Appropriations*

Occasionally a figure from a looted brass was set alongside new figures without alteration. The most striking example is the figure of John Wybarne (1503) at Ticehurst, Sussex, which is an appropriated knight of c.1380, twice the size of the wives beside him. The figures of Margaret Gill (c.1510) at Wyddial, Herts., and Thomas Andrewes (c.1510) at Charwelton, Northants., are only about thirty years earlier than the rest of the composition and are far less incongruous. More frequently a new inscription was added to an existing composition as at Horley, Surrey, altering the commemoration from 1420 to 1516, and at Bromham, Beds., from 1435 to 1535.

3. *Appropriations with alterations*

Appropriated figures were sometimes re-engraved to suit the changed fashion. Examples are rare. The finest is Walter Curson and family (c.1540) at Waterperry, Oxon., made from both altered and reversed portions of the brass of Simon Kamp (1442) from the Priory of the Holy Trinity, London (Fig. 118). Others are at Okeover, Staffs., and Great Ormsby, Norfolk. A particularly curious example is that of a civilian (c.1360) at Hampsthwaite, York., over whose body has been engraved an inscription to Ad Dyxon of 1571.

4. *True palimpsests*

The true palimpsest, in which the original engraving has

been erased and the obverse re-engraved, is very diffi-cult to detect. A clear example is the inscription of Sir Thomas Massyngberde (1552) at Gunby, Lincs., where in places both layers of lettering are readable. The reverse is also engraved, showing the brass to have been used on three occasions.

Most palimpsests are re-used brasses of local origin (Figs. 119,120). The London workshops were clearly full of monastic spoil by 1545, and the Norwich centres some-what earlier. The Flemish workshops were re-using ma-terials by 1570. Many of the brasses of this period are composed of a variety of fragments. Robert Barfott and family (1546) at Lambourne, Essex, is typical. The brass is made from a vowess (c.1460), a merchant (c.1445), a priest (c.1440), a large ecclesiastic (c.1440), a civilian (c.1370), a shield of arms (c.1500) and an Evangelist sym-bol (c.1500). Re-used fragments have been found as early as c.1300 at Pettaugh, Suffolk, and to within five years of the obverse as at Easton Neston, Northants. Some reveal portions of curious subjects, such as the monastic figure behind bars at St John Sepulchre, Norwich. Modern re-search is 'exposing' a large number of examples.

Not only the brasses were re-used. There are many examples of looted slabs being re-cut for the insertion of later brasses. The old indent occasionally appears below the new, as at Constantine, Cornwall. Many altar slabs have been desecrated in this manner and their consecra-tion crosses defaced. Continental palimpsests are found at Bruges, Ghent, Brussels, Sluys, Gouda and Lübeck.

Much continental loot was imported for re-engraving. Examples of re-used continental plate generally occur on brasses dated 1560 to 1585. A large amount of spoil from the Netherlands was imported into London during these years (Fig. 121). Apart from the reverses being of Fle-mish style, the continental provenance of some of the pieces has been established. The brass of Jacobus Weghenschede of Bergues St Winock is practically com-pleted by joining the reverses of brasses at Denham, Suf-folk (1574), and Yealmpton, Devon (1580). The base of the brass to Visch de la Chapelle which lay at St Donat, Bruges, has been found on the reverse of John Bonde and family (1578) at Thorpe, Surrey.

In addition to the intrinsic interest of the re-used pieces, the linking of various fragments from widely separated places has provided conclusive proof that brasses of cer-tain recognizable styles were made in central workshops, almost certainly in London and Norwich.

Not all engraving on the reverse of brasses is palimpsest

g. 121. Detail of sixteenth-century Flem-
ı reverse to inscription of Rowland Tail-
r, c. 1560. Hadleigh, Suffolk. 22" x 15½".

material. There are many cases of 'doodles' on the back
of brasses where apprentices practised. A very curious
example at Colby, Norfolk (1508), shows trial inscriptions and invocations squeezed on to the back of a scroll.
Elizabethan scratchings of circles, patterns, boots and
other queer objects are not uncommon. Nor were all looted brasses re-used as brasses. The engravers were not
specialists. At York Minster the inscription of John
Moore (1597) was turned into a weather-cock. A sundial
formerly at Bristol, signed by R. Treswell in 1582, was
cut from a Flemish shroud brass. Two unusual circular
brasses to fifteenth-century priests, re-engraved in the
seventeenth century with mathematical instruments, are
in the British Museum collection. In contrast, a copper-
plate engraving of an allegorical picture relating to the
Church of England, was re-engraved for the inscription
of Deborah Marks (1730) at Steeple Ashton, Wilts.

Many palimpsests are mounted so that both sides may
be inspected or rubbed. Other reverses have been cast
or electrotyped for the same purpose.

Brasses have suffered severely from the ravages and de-
mands of war. The magnificent French series was taken
up during the Revolution for the sake of the metal. The
Thirty Years War was fought across Germany with great
savagery, and many churches suffered. There has been
much recent destruction. Many of the brasses of Nieuport, Belgium, were destroyed between 1914 and 1918.
Losses were severe during the last World War. Brasses
destroyed in Germany include the Flemish brasses of
John Clingenberg (1356) and Tydemann Bercke (1521) at
Lübeck, a fourteenth-century Flemish priest at St Severin,
Cologne, a number of sixteenth-century plates from other
churches, and important fifteenth-century military
figures at Cleeves, Linnich and Hamm. In Poland the
magnificent brass of the fifteenth-century Flemish
school to Bishop Andreas and the brasses of the Vischer
atelier at Poznan and Samotuly have disappeared. Two
important episcopal brasses at Wroclaw have been badly
mutilated, and the precious group of Silesian dukes at
Lubiaz scattered and broken. In England the brasses of
the Swynbornes and Marnays at Little Horkesley, Essex,
and Sir Hugh Johnys and family at Swansea, have suffered mutilation. It is tragic that many of the continental
brasses were never rubbed.

Notwithstanding these disasters, the greatest destroyers
have been accident and neglect. Brasses, uncared for,
have worked loose and been stolen, or even sold by the
church. The recorded losses of the eighteenth and nine-

teenth centuries are appalling. The great series at Ingham, Norfolk, St George's Chapel, Windsor, St Alkmund's, Shrewsbury, King's Lynn, Norfolk, and many of the brasses in York Minster, are examples of loss through ignorance and neglect. The most tragic loss of all was the gorgeous array of monuments in St Donat and St Walburge, Bruges, which were regarded as scrap. Losses still occur. Very recently the brass of Hugh Johnson (1618) at Hackney, London, disappeared after a fire. Fortunately in many cases the slab with its indent has remained when the brass has gone. The evidence of such indents is particularly important in the case of separate inlay brasses, as the outlines usually reveal the nature of the brass with great exactness.

Some attempts have been made to restore lost or damaged brasses. The earliest English example is at Minster in Sheppey, where the legs of John de Northwood are a Tudor reconstruction. Queen Elizabeth I ordered that monuments should be respected and damage made good, though little action followed the direction. During the seventeenth century several restorations were carried out, promoted by the gentry out of regard for their ancestors. The brasses of the Bartelots at Stopham, Sussex, the Derings at Pluckley, Kent (Fig. 122), and the Fitzwilliams at Marholm, Northants., received extensive repair, including the replacement of whole figures. Modern restorations are more common, especially noteworthy being those at Tideswell and Chesterfield, Derbyshire, for the brasses of 1358 and 1519, Skipton, Yorks., for a brass of 1570, and Beddington, Surrey, for a brass of 1520. The Winchester College series was mostly restored following a modern theft. The extensive replacements at Cobham are less satisfactory, as errors in design and heraldry have been incorporated into the original work. The value of the restoration of brasses is a controversial matter, but the care of brasses is not. And a note on this topic makes a fitting conclusion. The damage of the past cannot be undone, but the fragments can be protected. All brasses should be protected from foot-tread by carpets or railing. Brasses which have been taken from their slabs and fixed to walls should be mounted on wood to prevent the chemical action of the limewash on the metal. Occasional cleaning with a paraffin rag is recommended. Cleaning with abrasive polishes is harmful, and covering with coconut matting particularly injurious. Loose brasses should be dealt with promptly and expertly. The Secretary of the Monumental Brass Society is always willing to give advice and assistance where possible.

Fig. 122. A restoration of the seventeen century for Richard Dering, 1545, at Pluc ley, Kent. Length 18".

It is hoped that the reader will be sufficiently interested to study this subject further. A large number of books and articles relevant to the study of brasses have been published, and the following are recommended.

The Brasses of England by H. W. Macklin (1907) is a well illustrated general treatise, and the best introduction. *Monumental Brasses* by the same author, reprinted in 1963 in a revised edition with a preface by C. Oman, includes county lists of places possessing brasses. The early text book *A Manual of Monumental Brasses* in two volumes by H. Haines (1861) is a most scholarly and informative work and remains a first class source. *A List of Monumental Brasses in the British Isles* by M. Stephenson (1926) with an appendix by M. S. Giuseppi and R. Griffin (1938) - the two have been re-published together in 1964 - is the authoritative list of English brasses A shorter list, classified according to types of costume, is given in the *Catalogue of Rubbings of Brasses and Incised Slabs,* second edition (1929), of the Victoria and Albert Museum.

The Transactions of the Monumental Brass Society, now in their tenth volume, record findings and opinions on every aspect of the subject. *Monumental Brasses* by Sir James Mann (1957), in the King Penguin Series, is a short introduction with a most authoritative section on military brasses.

There are other general books which can only be recommended for certain features. *Church Brasses* by A. C. Bouquet (1956) is a most interesting book, covering many unusual aspects of brasses, but it is marred by numerous errors of fact. *Brasses* by J. Franklyn (1964) includes a detailed chapter on the reading of inscriptions. *English Church Brasses from the Thirteenth to the Seventeenth Centuries* by E. R. Suffling (1910) is only valuable for its many unusual illustrations, especially of East Anglian brasses. *Ancient Memorial Brasses* by E. T. Beaumont (1913), *The Brasses of Our Homeland Churches* by W. E. Gawthorp (1923) and *Brasses* by J. S. Ward (1912) are elementary introductions.

The best sources of illustration are the *Portfolios of the Monumental Brass Society,* the *Oxford Portfolio of Monumental Brasses* (1898-1901), and the superb coloured engravings in *A Series of Monumental Brasses from the Thirteenth to the Seventeenth Century* by J. G. and L. A. R. Waller (1842-64). *Monumental Brasses and Slabs* (1847) and *The Monumental Brasses of England*

(1849) by C. Boutell contain a good selection of engravings. *A Manual of Costume as Illustrated in Monumental Brasses* by H. Druitt (1906) has a large number of illustrations, many being photographs of the actual brasses. The Victoria and Albert Museum Catalogue is excellently illustrated.

A large number of books and articles have been written on the brasses of particular counties, and practically all are recorded in Mill Stephenson's *List*, to which readers are referred. An authoritative series of articles are Mill Stephenson's own studies on Surrey, Shropshire and Yorkshire, and his description, in co-operation with R. Griffin, of Kent brasses. More recent publications of equal scholarship are on Somerset by A. B. Connor, in the *Proceedings of the Somerset Archaeological and Natural History Society*, and on Middlesex by Dr H. K. Cameron, now being published in the *Transactions of the London and Middlesex Archaeological Society*. Of the county books, *The Monumental Brasses of Wiltshire* by G. E. Kite (1860), *The Monumental Brasses of Cornwall* by E. H. W. Dunkin (1882), *Monumental Brasses of Gloucestershire* by C. T. Davis (1899), *The Monumental Brasses of Lancashire and Cheshire* by J. L. Thornley (1893) and *Monumental Brasses of Berkshire* by T. H. Morley (1924) are all comprehensive, though the first three have better texts. W. D. Belcher's *Kentish Brasses* in two volumes (1888 and 1905) is only interesting for its illustrations. The engravings by John Sell Cotman of Norfolk and Suffolk brasses (1819 and 1839) and by Thomas Fisher of Bedfordshire brasses (1828) are particularly valuable as a record of many lost memorials. Brasses on the Continent have not received such specialist attention. The only general treatise is *A Book of Facsimiles of Monumental Brasses on the Continent of Europe* by the Rev. W. F. Creeny (1884). This is a remarkable book which provides large illustrations and detailed information of many of Europe's finest brasses. The supplement to Creeny's work by R. H. Edleston in the *Report of the Peterborough Archaeological Society* (1932) adds only a few examples. The Monumental Brass Society Transactions and Portfolios have described and illustrated a great many, the most important articles being those of R. Pearson, F. A. Greenhill and J. Belonje on brasses from Flanders and the Rhineland, F. A. Greenhill on brasses from Norway, and H. K. Cameron, H. F. Owen Evans and the author on German brasses. The only major record of French brasses is the drawings of François-Roger de Gaignières at the Bibliothèque Nationale, Paris, and the Bodleian Library, Oxford.

An excellent summary of the Flemish workshops is made by S. Collon-Gevaert in *Histoire des Arts du Métal en Belgique*, Brussels (1951). The problems surrounding the fourteenth-century Flemish school and its products are fully discussed by the German authority H. Eichler in *Die Gravierten Grabplatten aus Metall im XIV Jahrhundert und ihre Vorstufen*, Cologne (1933). An illustrated description of brasses in Belgium forms part of the *Catalogue Descriptif-Frottis de Tombes Plates*, Brussels (1912), by H. Rousseau. A large number of destroyed Flemish brasses are engraved in *Inscriptions Funéraires et Monumentales de la Flandre Occidentale* by J. Gaillard, Bruges (1866).

German brasses in Saxony, especially those from the Vischer foundry, have been well described. *Peter Vischer der Ältere und seine Werkstatt* by S. Meller, Leipzig (1925), is a standard work on the Vischers. *Metallne Grabplatten in Sachsen* by J. Kramer, Halle (1912), is a secondary source. H. Gerlach in *Die Mittelalterlichen gravierten messingen Grabplatten in der Domen zu Meissen und Freiberg*, Freiberg (1866), deals specifically with the Meissen and Freiberg brasses. Northern and western Germany is covered by the articles already mentioned.

Many Polish brasses have been described in Polish by Polish authorities. The Poznan brasses by the Vischers are discussed by Meller. The brasses of Krakow are illustrated and described by F. Kopera in *Monuments de Cracowie*, Krakow (1904). Many of the Silesian brasses are described by H. Luchs in *Schlesische Fürstenbilder des Mittelalters*, Breslau (1868).

The following books and articles deal with special aspects of the study of brasses.

A Manual of Costume as Illustrated in Monumental Brasses by H. Druitt (1906) is the standard work on costume, but now needs revision.

A valuable experiment in the classification of brasses according to style is J. P. C. Kent's 'Monumental Brasses, a New Classification of Military Effigies' in the *Journal of the British Archaeological Association, XII*, 1949.

Three articles in the *Monumental Brass Society Transactions* deserve special mention. 'The Sculptor and the Brass' by Mrs. A. J. K. Esdaile (*M.B.S., Vol. VII*, 1935) deals with several identified engravers. 'The Metals Used in Monumental Brasses' by H. K. Cameron (*M.B.S., Vol. VIII*, 1946) is a detailed analysis of this technical subject. 'The Ledger of Andrew Halyburton' by F. A. Greenhill (*M.B.S., Vol. IX*, 1954) describes a unique record of

Scottish trade with Flanders in brasses and incised slabs. A knowledge of incised slabs is valuable to the student of brasses. The two major works on slabs are *The Incised Slabs of Leicestershire and Rutland* by F. A. Greenhill (1958), which includes a manual of British slabs, and *Illustrations of Incised Slabs on the Continent of Europe* by the Rev. W. F. Creeny (1891).

7 LIST OF OUTSTANDING BRASSES

The following lists are given for the easy reference of those looking for choice brasses. They do not pretend to be complete, but include the best examples. The letter M denotes a military figure, C a civilian, and E an ecclesiastical figure. An asterisk is placed against the finest brasses.

BEDFORDSHIRE
Aspley Guise, E, 1410. Bromham, M, 1435. Cardington, M, 1540. Cople, C, 1410; C, 1544. Elstow, E, 1520. Eyworth, C, 1624. Marston Morteyne, M, 1451. Shillington, E, 1400. Wymington, C, 1391; M, 1430. Good selections of brasses are at Ampthill, Cople, Dunstable, Hatley Cockayne and Luton. The series at Cople and Luton are particularly important.

BERKSHIRE
Bray, M, 1378 (bracket). Childrey, M, 1444*. Shottesbrooke C and E, 1370; C, 1401. Sparsholt, E, 1353. Wantage, M, 1414. West Hanney, E, 1370. Windsor, St George's Chapel, E, 1522. Good selections of brasses are at Blewbury, Bray, Childrey, Faringdon, Lambourn, Little Wittenham, Sonning, Wantage and West Hanney. The Childrey series is particularly fine. Brass rubbing is only permitted under exceptional circumstances at St George's Chapel, Windsor.

BUCKINGHAMSHIRE
Chenies, C, 1510. Denham, E, 1540. Drayton Beauchamp, M, 1368; M, 1375. Edlesborough, E, 1395. Eton, College Chapel, E, 1503. Middle Claydon, M, 1542. Over Winchendon, E, 1502. Pitstone, C, 1320. Stoke Poges, M, 1425. Taplow, C, 1350 (cross); C, 1455. Thornton, M, 1472*. Twyford, M, 1550. Waddesdon, M, 1490. Good selections are at Chalfont St Giles, Chalfont St Peter, Chenies, Denham, Dinton, Eton, Penn, Quainton, Waddesdon and Wooburn.

CAMBRIDGESHIRE
Balsham, E, 1401*; E, 1462*. Burwell, E, 1542. Cambridge, St John's College, E, 1414. Cambridge, Trinity Hall, E, 1517. Ely, Cathedral, E, 1554; E, 1614. Fulbourne, E, 1391. Hildersham, C, 1379 (cross); M, 1466. Horseheath, M, 1365. Isleham, M, 1484. Little Shelford, M, 1410. Trumpington, M, 1289*. Westley Waterless, M, 1325*. Wilburton, E, 1477. Wisbech, M, 1401. Wood Ditton, M, 1393. Good selections are at King's College Cambridge, Hildersham, Isleham and Little Shelford.

CHESHIRE
Macclesfield, C, 1506. Wilmslow, M, 1460.

CORNWALL
East Anthony, C, 1420. Lanteglos by Fowey, M, 1440. St Mellion, M, 1551. Good collections are at St Columb Major, Crowan, Mawgan in Pyder and St Michael Penkevil.

CUMBERLAND
Carlisle, Cathedral, E, 1496. Edenhall, M, 1458.

DERBYSHIRE
Ashbourne, M, 1538. Morley, M, 1481. Mugginton, M, 1485. Norbury, C, 1538 (palimpsest). Tideswell, E, 1579. Good selections are at Hathersage and Morley.

DEVONSHIRE
Dartmouth, St Saviour, M, 1408. Exeter, Cathedral, E, 1413. Stoke Fleming, C, 1391. A good selection is at Haccombe.

DORSET
Thorncombe, C, 1436. Wimborne Minster (King) 1440. Yetminster, M, 1531.

DURHAM
Sedgefield, C, 1330.

ESSEX
Aveley, M, 1370. Bowers Gifford, M, 1348. Chigwell, E, 1631*. Chrishall, M, 1370*. Dagenham, C, 1479. Great Bromley, E, 1432. Gosfield, C, 1440. Halstead, M, 1409. Ingrave, M, 1528. Little Easton, M, 1483*. Little Horkesley, M, 1412*; M, 1549. Pebmarsh, M, 1323*. Wimbish, M, 1347. Wivenhoe, M, 1507*; C, 1537. Good selections are at Barking, Brightlingsea, Harlow, Latton, Roydon, Saffron Walden, Stifford, Tilty, Tolleshunt Darcy, Upminster and Writtle.

GLOUCESTERSHIRE
Bristol, St Mary Redcliffe, C, 1439; C, 1480. Chipping Campden, C, 1401*. Cirencester, M, 1438; C, 1440*. Deerhurst, C, 1400*. Dyrham, M, 1401. Gloucester, St Mary de Crypt, C, 1544. Northleach, C, 1400; C, 1447; C, 1458*. Quinton, C, 1430. Winterbourne, C, 1370. Wormington, C, 1605. Wotton-under-Edge, M, 1392. Good selections are at Bristol St Mary Redcliffe, Chipping Campden, Cirencester, Fairford and Northleach, those at Cirencester and Northleach being especially important. The interesting brasses at St Peter and the Temple Church, Bristol, disappeared after the bombing of the churches, but the latter have been replaced in St Mary Redcliffe.

HAMPSHIRE
Crondall, E, 1381. Havant, E, 1413. King's Sombourne, C, 1380. Ringwood, E, 1416. Stoke Charity, M, 1482. Thruxton, M, 1425*. Winchester, St Cross, E, 1382. There are good collections at Odiham, Sherbourne St John, and in the chapel and cloisters of Winchester College (the brasses in the chapel are facsimiles).

HEREFORDSHIRE
Clehonger, M, 1470. Hereford, Cathedral, E, 1360*; E, 1386 (cross); M, 1435; E, 1529. The group of brasses in Hereford Cathedral is large and interesting.

HERTFORDSHIRE
Aldbury, M, 1547. Broxbourne, M, 1473. Digswell, M, 1415. Furneux Pelham, C, 1420. Great Berkhampstead, C, 1356. Hemel Hempstead, M, 1390. Hinxworth, C, 1487. Hunsdon, C, 1495. Knebworth, E, 1414. North Mymms, E, 1360. St Alban's Cathedral, E, 1360*; St Michael's, C, 1340; C, 1400 (cross). Sawbridgeworth, M, 1433. Watford, C, 1415. Watton at Stone, M, 1361; E, 1370. Wyddial, C, 1575. Good collections are at Aldenham, Clothall, Digswell, Great Berkhampstead, Hitchin, North Mymms, St Alban's Cathedral and Sawbridgeworth. The series at Sawbridgeworth and the monastic brasses in St Alban's cathedral are particularly interesting.

HUNTINGDONSHIRE
Diddington, M, 1505. Sawtry, M, 1404.

ISLE OF WIGHT
Freshwater, M, 1367.

KENT
Addington, M, 1409. Ashford, C, 1375. Bobbing, M, 1420. Brabourne, M, 1434. Chartham, M, 1306*. Cobham (the finest series of brasses in England from 1320 to 1529 with eighteen examples, mostly large**). Dartford, C, 1402. East Sutton, M, 1638*. East Wickham, C, 1325 (cross). Faversham, C, 1533. Graveney, C, 1436*. Herne, M, 1420. Hever, C, 1419; M, 1538*. Hoo St Werburgh, E, 1412. Horsmonden, E, 1340. Kemsing, E, 1320. Lydd, C, 1430. Maidstone, All Saints, C, 1593. Mereworth, M, 1366. Minster in Sheppey, M, 1330*; C, 1335*. Northfleet, E, 1375. Otterden, M, 1408. Saltwood, M, 1437. Seal, M, 1395. Sheldwich, M, 1394. Stone, E, 1408 (cross). Ulcombe, M, 1419; M, 1470. Upper Hardres, E, 1405 (bracket). Woodchurch, E, 1330 (cross). Good collections are at Addington, Ash next Sandwich, Biddenden, Birchington, Chartham, Cobham, Dartford, Faversham, Goudhurst, Great Chart, Herne, Hoo St Werburgh, Lydd, Margate, Newington juxta Hythe, Pluckley, Southfleet, Westerham and Wrotham.
Kent is the richest county in figure brasses in England. Brass rubbing is not, at present, allowed at Cobham or Westerham.

LANCASHIRE
Ormskirk, M, 1500. Sefton, M, 1570. Winwick, M, 1492; M, 1527. Good collections are at Manchester Cathedral and Middleton.

LEICESTERSHIRE
Bottesford, E, 1404*. Castle Donnington, M, 1458. Sibson, E, 1532. Stokerston, M, 1467; M, 1493. Thurcaston, E, 1425. Wanlip, M, 1393.

LINCOLNSHIRE
Barton on Humber, St Mary, C, 1433. Boston, C, 1398; E, 1400. Broughton, M, 1390. Buslingthorpe, M, 1300. Croft, M, 1300. Edenham, E, 1500. Gedney, C, 1390. Grainthorpe, 1380 (cross). Gunby, M, 1405; C, 1419. Irnham, M, 1390. Laughton, M, 1400. Linwood, C, 1419*; C, 1421. Norton Disney, M, 1578. Spilsby, C, 1391; M, 1410*. Stamford All Saints, C, 1460; C, 1460. Tattershall, M, 1455; C, 1470; C, 1475*; E, 1510. There is an excellent selection of brasses at Tattershall, and fragments of brasses at Boston.

LONDON
(City and Westminster) All Hallows Barkying, C, 1533. Westminster Abbey, E, 1395; E, 1397*; C, 1399*; M, 1437; E. 1498. There are good selections of brasses at All Hallows Barkyng, Great St Helen's, Bishopsgate and Westminster Abbey.

LONDON
(Former Middlesex) Enfield, C, 1470*. Fulham, C, 1529. Harrow, M, 1390; E, 1468. Hillingdon, M, 1509. Good selections of brasses are at Hackney, Hadley, Harefield, Harrow, Hayes, Hillingdon and Willesden. The interesting brasses at Isleworth have been dispersed and partly lost since a fire. The series at Harrow is particularly fine, but rubbing is not allowed.

NORFOLK
Blickling, M, 1401. Burnham Thorpe, M, 1420. Bylaugh, M, 1471. Elsing, M, 1347*. Erpingham, M, 1415. Felbrigg, M & C, 1380; M, 1416*. Great Fransham, M, 1414. Holme next the Sea, C, 1405. Hunstanton, M, 1506*. Ketteringham, M, 1499. Kings Lynn, C, 1349*; C, 1364*. Methwold, M, 1367. Narburgh, C, 1545. Norwich, St George Colegate, C, 1472 (bracket); St John Maddermarket, C, 1524 (bracket); St Lawrence, E, 1437. Reepham, M, 1391. Rougham, M, 1472. Shernbourne, M, 1458. Southacre, M, 1384. Upwell, E, 1430. Good selections of brasses are at Aldborough, Aylsham, Bawburgh, Blickling, Brampton, Cley, Felbrigg, Frenze, Loddon, Narborough, Necton, Norwich, St John Maddermarket (this series is particularly interesting), St Lawrence, St Stephen and Rougham.

NORTHAMPTONSHIRE
Ashby St Legers, M, 1506. Brampton Ash., M, 1420. Castle Ashby, E, 1401. Charwelton, C, 1490. Cotterstock, E, 1420 (bracket). Easton Neston, M, 1552. Greens Norton, M, 1462. Higham Ferrers, E, 1337*; 1400 (cross); C, 1425. Nether Heyford M, 1487. Lowick, M, 1467. Newton by Geddington, C, 1400 (cross). Rothwell, E, 1361. Good selections of brasses are at Ashby St Legers, Higham Ferrers, Wappenham and Warkworth. The Higham Ferrers series is of outstanding interest.

NORTHUMBERLAND
Newcastle-upon-Tyne, All Saints, C, 1429*. This splendid brass is covered by plate glass.

NOTTINGHAMSHIRE
East Markham, C, 1419. Holme Pierre-Pont, C, 1380. Newark, C, 1361*. Strelley, M, 1487. Wollaton, M, 1471.

OXFORDSHIRE
Brightwell Baldwin, C, 1439. Cassington, 1414 (cross). Checkendon, C, 1404. Chinnor, E, 1320 (cross). Ewelme, M, 1436. Great Tew, M, 1410. Mapledurham, M, 1395. Oxford, Merton College Chapel, E, 1320; E, 1420 (bracket); E, 1471. New College Chapel, E, 1417*. Rotherfield Greys, M, 1387. Thame, M, 1460. Good selections of brasses are at Chinnor, Chipping Norton, Dorchester, Oxford, Christchurch Cathedral, Magdalen College Chapel, Merton College Chapel and the Queens College Chapel, New College Chapel, Thame and Waterperry. The series at Chinnor and New College Chapel, Oxford, are of outstanding interest. Rubbing of the 1320 Chinnor brass is not at present allowed.

RUTLAND
Little Casterton, M, 1410.

SHROPSHIRE
Acton Burnell, M, 1382. Adderley, E, 1390. Ightfield, C, 1495. Tong, M, 1467*.

SOMERSET
Ilminster, M, 1440; M, 1618*. St Decumans, M, 1596. South Petherton, M, 1430.

STAFFORDSHIRE
Audley, M, 1385. Norbury, C, 1360. Okeover, M, 1447.

SUFFOLK
Acton, M, 1302*; C, 1435. Barsham, M, 1415. Burgate, M, 1409. Gorleston, M, 1320. Letheringham, M, 1389. Mendlesham, M, 1417. Playford, M, 1400. Stoke by Nayland, M, 1408. Yoxford, C, 1485. Good selections are at Brundish, Euston, Ipswich St Mary Tower, Long Melford, Orford, Sotterley, Stoke by Nayland and Yoxford.

SURREY
Beddington, C, 1432. East Horsley, E, 1478. Horley, C, 1420. Lingfield, M, 1403. Stoke D'Abernon, M, 1277*; M, 1327*. Good selections are at Beddington, Camberwell St Giles, Carshalton. Cheam, Lingfield, Merstham, Shere and Thames Ditton. The series at Lingfield is particularly important. Several Surrey brasses are under glass as at Byfleet, Cobham and Oakwood.

SUSSEX
Ardingly, C, 1500. Arundel, M, 1430. Broadwater, E, 1432; 1445 (cross). Buxted, E, 1408 (cross). Clapham, M, 1526. Cowfold, E, 1433*. Etchingham, M, 1388; M, 1444. Fletching, M, 1380. Hurstmonceux, M, 1402. Trotton, C, 1310*; M, 1419*. Warbleton, E, 1436. West Grinstead, M, 1441. Wiston, M, 1426. Good selections are at Ardingly, Arundel, Battle and West Firle.

WARWICKSHIRE
Baginton, M, 1407. Merevale, M, 1413. Warwick, St Mary, M, 1406*. Wixford, M, 1411*. There is a good selection at the chapel of Compton Verney House, but these can only be seen by appointment. The St. Mary, Warwick, brasses are placed at an extremely difficult height for rubbing.

WILTSHIRE
Cliffe Pypard, M, 1380. Dauntsey, C, 1539. Draycot Cerne, M, 1393. Fovant, E, 1492. Mere, M, 1398. Salisbury Cathedral, E, 1375*.

WORCESTERSHIRE
Fladbury, M, 1445. Kidderminster, M, 1415. Strensham, M, 1390; M, 1405. Good selections are at Fladbury, Strensham and Tredington.

YORKSHIRE
Aldborough, M, 1360. Brandsburton, M, 1397. Cottingham, E, 1383. Harpham, M, 1418. Topcliffe, C, 1391. Wensley, E, 1360*. York, Minster, E, 1315.

In London, the British Museum, the Victoria and Albert Museum and the Society of Antiquaries have large collections of brasses. Collections are held by the Cambridge Museum of Archaeology, the Northants Antiquarian Society, the Norwich St Peter Hungate Museum and the Surrey Archaeological Society, Guildford. The very fine brass to Thomas Pownder (1525) from St Mary Quay, Ipswich, is now in the Ipswich Museum.

The following notable brasses can be found outside the English Counties, in Great Britain and in Ireland.

WALES
Beaumaris, Anglesey, C, 1530. Llanbeblig, Carnarvon, C, 1500. Llanwrst, Denbigh (six 17th-century brasses). Swansea, Glamorgan, M, 1500. The Llanwryst brasses are under glass.

SCOTLAND
Aberdeen, St Nicholas, C, 1613. Edinburgh, St Giles 1569 (inscription). Glasgow, Cathedral, M, 1605.

IRELAND
Dublin, St Patrick's, E, 1528; E, 1537; C, 1579.

Important recorded continental brasses are found in the following places.

BELGIUM
Antwerp, Mayer van den Bergh Museum, E; Bruges, Béguinage, E, Cathedral of St Sauveur, M, E, C*, St Jacques C*, Hospice St Jean, ins., Hospice St Josse, E, Archaeological Museum, ins.; Brussels, Musées Royaux du Cinquantenaire, M*; Crombeke, ins.; Damme, Hospital of St John, E; Dendermonde, E; Dixmude, C; Ghent, Museum de Bijloke, M and E; Mechlin, museum, M; Nieuportville, C; Nivelles, E; Thielen, M; Tournai, E; Ypres, Hospital St Jean ins.; Vichte, C.

DENMARK
Ringstead, king*.

FINLAND
Nausis, E*.

FRANCE
Amiens, cathedral, E; Haute Vienne, St Junien, E; Bordeaux, museum, C; Paris, the Louvre, C.

GERMANY, WEST
Aachen, cathedral, E; Altenberg, M; Bardowijk, E; Brauweilers, E; Bremen, cathedral, E; Cologne, Diocesan museum, C; Constance, E*; Cues, E; Emden, E*; Hildesheim, cathedral, E; Lübeck, cathedral, E*, Marienkirche, C*, St Catherine's, C*, St Anne Museum, C; Paderborn, cathedral, E; Verden, St Andrew, E*; Xanten, E.

GERMANY, EAST
Altenburg, castle chapel, C; Erfurt, cathedral, E; Freiberg, C and M*; Fürstenwalde, E; Gadebusch, queen; Halberstadt, cathedral, E; Meissen, cathedral, M and C*; Naumburg, E; Nordhausen, C; Schwerin, E*; Stolberg, C; Stralsund, St Nicholas, C*; Torgau, C; Zeitz, castle chapel, E. Nordhausen was very badly damaged in the last war and the survival of the brasses in the hospital of St Chriaci has not been established by the author.

HOLLAND
Alkmaar, C; Breda, E; Gouda; Nymwegen, C; Zevenaar, altarpiece.

ITALY
Susa, altarpiece.

NORWAY
Oslo, University museum, M.

MADEIRA
Funchal, C.

POLAND
Krakow, cathedral, E*; Czarnkow, M; Gniezno, E; Nowemiasto, M*; Lubiaz, M*; Poznan, cathedral, E; Tomice, M; Torun, St John, C*; Wielgomblyny, M; Wroclaw, cathedral, E, Holy Cross church, E, St Elizabeth, ins., Diocesan museum, E. Portions of the Lubiaz brasses are in the Wroclaw Archaeological museum.

PORTUGAL
Coimbra, ins.; Evora, C; Leça do Balio, ins.

SPAIN
Avila, E; Madrid, Archaeological museum, C*; Seville, Archaeological museum, C, University chapel, M.

SWEDEN
Vester Åker, C.

SWITZERLAND
Basel museum, M.

In conclusion, the reader's attention is drawn to the Monumental Brass Society. This society, formed specifically to help in the preservation and investigation of brasses, is receiving and seeking an increased membership. Original research is welcome in its transactions. The address of the Honorary Secretary is:

        c/o The Society of Antiquaries,
        Burlington House,
        London, W.1.

to whom enquiries should be made.

SUBJECT INDEX

ACKNOWLEDGEMENTS

The author has received considerable help from many friends in the writing of this book. Special acknowledgement is made to H. J. B. Allen, H. T. Norris and I. T. W. Shearman for invaluable help in making many of the rubbings illustrated, and to F. A. Greenhill, F.S.A., Major H. F. Owen Evans, M.B.E., F.S.A., and J. C. Page-Phillips for information relating to the text.

Most of the rubbings illustrated are from the author's collection. Thanks are recorded to Major H. F. Owen Evans for the rubbings illustrated in figs. 18, 47, 106, 111, 112 and 113, and to J. C. Page-Phillips and R. Greenwood for the rubbings shown in figs. 36, 85 and 86. Acknowledgement is made to the Oxford University Archaeological Society for fig. 117, a reproduction from their portfolio.

Figs. 28 and 68 are taken from *A Series of Monumental Brasses* by J. G. and L. A. R. Waller, 1864, and figs. 12 and 71 from *A Book of Facsimiles of Monumental Brasses on the Continent of Europe* by the Rev. W. F. Creeny, 1884. Acknowledgements and thanks are given to the Monumental Brass Society for permission to use reproductions from their portfolios and transactions for figs. 23, 51, 77 and 109.

Most of the rubbings have been photographed by A. and E. Wright of Stansted Mountfitchet, Essex. Figs. 8 and 74 are by Vitachrome, High Street, Kensington, London, fig. 27 by G. Burnett and fig. 78 by H. J. B. Allen.

Appreciation is recorded of the help given by many friends in a variety of ways, especially by J. and E. Pritchard and my wife, and by all the clergy who, by their courtesy, have made this book possible.